THE NEW METRICS

THE NEW METRICS: PRACTICAL ASSESSMENT OF RESEARCH IMPACT

EDITED BY

ELAINE M. LASDA
University at Albany, USA

United Kingdom – North America – Japan – India – Malaysia – China

Emerald Publishing Limited
Howard House, Wagon Lane, Bingley BD16 1WA, UK

First edition 2019

Copyright © 2019 Emerald Publishing Limited

Reprints and permissions service
Contact: permissions@emeraldinsight.com

No part of this book may be reproduced, stored in a retrieval system, transmitted in any form or by any means electronic, mechanical, photocopying, recording or otherwise without either the prior written permission of the publisher or a licence permitting restricted copying issued in the UK by The Copyright Licensing Agency and in the USA by The Copyright Clearance Center. Any opinions expressed in the chapters are those of the authors. Whilst Emerald makes every effort to ensure the quality and accuracy of its content, Emerald makes no representation implied or otherwise, as to the chapters' suitability and application and disclaims any warranties, express or implied, to their use.

British Library Cataloguing in Publication Data
A catalogue record for this book is available from the British Library

ISBN: 978-1-78973-270-2 (Print)
ISBN: 978-1-78973-269-6 (Online)
ISBN: 978-1-78973-271-9 (Epub)
ISBN: 978-1-78973-272-6 (Pbk.)

INVESTOR IN PEOPLE

Contents

Acknowledgements — vi

About the Contributors — vii

Chapter 1 A Brief History and Overview
Elaine M. Lasda — *1*

Chapter 2 Scholarly Metrics at NCAR
Keith Maull and Matthew Mayernik — *15*

Chapter 3 New Metrics for Measuring Academic Research Outside the Ivory Tower
Kendra K. Levine — *39*

Chapter 4 A Breath of Fresh Air: New Bibliometric Services at EPA-RTP Library
Anthony Holderied and Taylor Abernethy Johnson — *59*

Chapter 5 Compliance and Defiance: Michigan Publishing's Early Encounters with Research Impact Metrics
Rebecca Welzenbach and Charles Watkinson — *93*

Chapter 6 Altmetrics in the Museum Environment
Richard P. Hulser — *115*

Chapter 7 What Have We Learned Today? A Synthesis of Cases Presented
Elaine M. Lasda — *131*

Index — *141*

Acknowledgements

The editor wishes to acknowledge the hard work and dedication of the chapter contributors, Emerald Publishing staff, as well as the experience, influence, and mentorship of Special Libraries Association members, past, future, and present, without whom this book would not exist.

About the Contributors

Taylor Abernethy Johnson is a Durham, North Carolina, native currently working as the User Services and Research Librarian (University of North Carolina [UNC] Contractor) at the US Environmental Protection Agency Library in Research Triangle Park, North Carolina. She holds the responsibility of managing the library's Interlibrary Loan Department along with several reference capacities including contributing to the development of a new Research Impact Services Program. Taylor earned an MSLS from UNC's School of Information and Library Science in Fall 2016.

Anthony Holderied is the Assistant Director of the Environmental Protection Agency Library at Research Triangle Park (EPA-RTP), North Carolina. Under contract with the School of Information and Library Science at the University of North Carolina at Chapel Hill, he has overseen several key research service areas at EPA-RTP Library since 2013. Holderied holds an MLS and MA in educational media and has published in the fields of information literacy, assessment, instructional design, and bibliometrics.

Richard P. Hulser, MEd, MLS, is President of Richard P. Hulser Consulting and Fellow of the Special Libraries Association. His expertise includes altmetrics implementation in a museum, library and archives assessment and implementation, content digitization and licensing, and vendor partnerships in academic, corporate, and cultural environments.

Elaine M. Lasda is Associate Librarian at the University at Albany (UAlbany), SUNY, where she is primary point person on scholarly impact metrics. As the Social Welfare Subject Specialist, she also liaises with the university's School of Social Welfare. She received her MLS from UAlbany and a master's-level certificate in data science from Syracuse University. She received the SUNY Chancellor's Award for Excellence in Librarianship in 2015. She has written articles for the *Journal of Academic Librarianship*, *Reference Services Review*, *Information Outlook*, and *Online Searcher*, among others. She frequently presents on topics such as research impact, data literacy, and open access.

Kendra K. Levine is the Director of the Institute of Transportation Studies Library at the University of California, Berkeley. She manages library operations, provides research support for transportation faculty, students, and professionals across California, and works with the transportation research community to make research accessible. Kendra earned a Masters of Library and Information Science and a Masters of Information Systems from Drexel University in 2006.

Keith Maull is Software Engineer and Data Scientist at the National Center for Atmospheric Research (NCAR). His work focuses on initiatives for gathering and analyzing metrics that illustrate the impact of NCAR's scientific activities. His research interests are scholarly metrics, open science, reproducible computational research, and supporting platforms for data curation and analysis. He received his Master's and PhD in Computer Science from the University of Colorado at Boulder.

Matthew Mayernik is Project Scientist and Research Data Service Specialist in the National Center for Atmospheric Research (NCAR) Library. He received his Master's and PhD from the University of California, Los Angeles, Department of Information Studies. His work is focused on research and service development related to scientific data curation. His research interests include metadata practices and standards, data citation and identity, and social and institutional aspects of research data. He is a member of the Board on Data Stewardship within the American Meteorological Society.

Charles Watkinson is Director of University of Michigan Press and Associate University Librarian for Publishing at the University of Michigan Library. He is responsible for the publishing division of the Library which includes the Press, Michigan Publishing Services, and the Deep Blue repository and research data services.

Rebecca Welzenbach is the Research Impact Librarian at the University of Michigan Library, where she helps scholars communicate the importance of their work and coordinates the library's role in research impact activities on campus. She earned her MSI from the University of Michigan School of Information in 2009.

Chapter 1

A Brief History and Overview

Elaine M. Lasda

Data-driven. Evidence-based. Outcome-oriented. Common buzzwords abound today that show our propensity as a society for (generally) quantifiable, numerical information that will enable decision-making, allocation of resources, and viability of initiatives and projects. Traditionally, the measure of scientific achievement is based on where and when research output is subsequently cited in other scholarship, generally peer-reviewed journal articles (PRJAs). Citation-based metrics, known as bibliometrics, are now bolstered by other indicators such as alternative metrics, web analytics, journal usage metrics, and other measures of productivity, reach, impact, prestige, and so forth. The existence of these broader measures of research impact has been largely facilitated by electronic publishing and dissemination of scholarly thought and output electronically and on the World Wide Web. Use of metrics such as the Journal Impact Factor (JIF), citation counts, and more recently, the *h*-index have primarily been utilized in academic tenure and promotion dossiers to demonstrate the success or merit of the candidate's scholarly pursuits. Evaluation of research through measures of impact extends beyond academe, and use of these indicators is manifesting in new places and in new ways. This work presents five case studies that show how a variety of research impact indicators are being used in specialized settings.

First, providing a bit about the context, history, and evolution of research impact metrics will help set the stage for each of our organizations and lend clarity to their use of metrics in organizational activities.

A Matter of Resource Allocation

Government funding is a key support for scientific inquiry in the United States. Nonetheless, according to the American Association for the Advancement of Science, the allocation of all Federal R&D funds peaked at 11.7% of the total US budget in 1965, but by 2017 all R&D funding represented a mere 2.9% of the Federal budget (American Association for the Advancement of Science, 2018). This exemplifies the ever-increasing scarcity of resources available for so-called "pure science," that is, phenomena studied "without regard to practical applications" (Stevenson, 2010).

Resources have decreased, disciplinary subspecialties have increased, as has overall research output. There is a need for scrutiny of research pursuits, as we have seen from well-known retracted theorems such as the vaccine-autism scare and the viability of cold fusion (Institute of Medicine, 2004; Ritter, 2003). Thus, it may be only natural that funders of scientific pursuits seek additional means of distinguishing among project applications.

The resultant need for scientists and researchers to justify and promote their research agenda with funders and other constituencies has engendered a variety of metrics from which to evaluate research at all unit levels: article, author, research group, institution, discipline, country, so on. Part of the reason for this proliferation is that we can now collect and analyze data on a scale heretofore unprecedented, and there are increasingly sophisticated means of analyzing and discerning patterns (Nowakowska, 1990; Raan, 2014).

There is a rapidly shifting landscape when it comes to measures of research impact. For decades after Eugene Garfield first conceived of his citation index schema, its strength was primarily in coverage of the hard sciences. It has long been the case that social sciences coverage in Garfield's Social Science Citation Index was significantly less robust, and arts and humanities coverage was even further wanting. Nonetheless, it was the only source with citation data considered authoritative until the early 2000s, when competitors Scopus and Google Scholar began to also provide citation indexing. Clarivate Analytics (2017), the current corporate owner of the Institute for Scientific Information (ISI) indexes appears to be both actively and proactively working to assure Web of Science retains its dominant position in the research impact metrics domain by adding journal titles and new databases that cover books, datasets, emerging journals, and more.

For better or worse, quantitative and qualitative measures are being used to evaluate research and scholarship of all stripes, despite limitations to various indicators. Experts in bibliometrics, altmetrics, and general measures of scholarly reach have long documented the pitfalls of over-reliance and irresponsible use of research impact and metrics indicators (Wilsdon et al., 2015).

Probably the main concern about indicators of scholarly impact for evaluative purposes is that it creates an incentive to play to the metric or, as Muller (2018) calls it "juke the stats" (p. 2). The premise is thus: due to the research cycle reward system of increased funding and support for researchers with high research impact scores of varying ilk, scholars will direct their research inquiries toward areas that garner attention or are hot topics, than toward lines of inquiry that are just as, if not more important than the high profile research but may be seen as dry or a fringe area undeserving of attention at the current juncture.

Major Influencers and Sources of Today's Research Impact Metrics

Additional context related to the current metrics landscape is provided by a brief introduction of significant contributions and contributors to the scientometric landscape.

The use of the term "bibliometrics" is widely attributed to Alan Pritchard. Pritchard felt it was necessary to identify a term of art for this burgeoning field. He defined bibliometrics as "...the application of mathematics and statistical methods to books and other media of communication" (p. 348). An interesting side note: Pritchard would have preferred the term "scientology," which he felt would be a clear term implying the study of science. Unfortunately that term was by that time already in use by the religious group founded by L. Ron Hubbard (Pritchard, 1969).

"Documentation through the association of ideas, " and the influence of such tools as library authority tables and the legal field's *Shepard's Citations* drove Eugene Garfield's conceptualization of a citation-based scientific index (Garfield in Cronin & Sugimoto, 2015). Garfield's contributions to bibliometrics, citation indexing, and scientometrics are well documented; for a brief but inclusive summary, see Lawler's (2014) chapter in *The Future of the History of Chemical Information*. Garfield's ISI expanded the citation index repertoire to social sciences, arts, and humanities. After being an independent for-profit entity, ISI has been subsumed by a firm called Clarivate, by way of an intermediate acquisition by Thomson Reuters, and the citation indexes were renamed Web of Science along the way. The indicators contained in Web of Science are citation-based and well known. Garfield remains revered for his vision and drive in conceiving and executing the Science Citation Index and later indexes for other disciplines. Many a written work extolls his brilliance and vision; in fact, Cronin and Atkins (2000) collected and edited a volume of devoted papers and essays largely singing his praises. There has not been merely this reverential treatment. Cronin, 15 years after the publication of his *Festschrift,* this time with collaborator Cassidy Sugimoto, compiled an even more ponderous tome of articles and essays expounding on historical and current concerns related to the use and misuse of scholarly metrics (Cronin & Sugimoto, 2015). As regards Garfield, one presupposes it is best to separate the man from the metrics. Aside from citation counts, the JIF, an unweighted ratio of times cited over articles published for a two-year or five-year time frame is the main metric associated with Web of Science. Cited Half-life, and Immediacy Index, also original metrics of Garfield's, are measures of the length of a reference's viability over time and the speed by which the reference gets traction and spreads, respectively. More recently, Web of Science added Eigenfactor, a weighted ratio based on the premise that some citing references have greater influence or value than others, and the Article Influence Score which corrects the Eigenfactor Score to a per article-level metric. Eigenfactor and Article Influence calculations were inspired by Google's PageRank methodology (Bergstrom, 2007).

Scopus

Scopus was launched in 2004 by Elsevier with a larger set of covered publications than Web of Science, user-friendly navigability, and expert review panels. At the time of its release, Scopus was less expensive than Web of Science, easy to use, and retained quality control through a panel of experts reviewing journal content.

Others have documented the errors and omissions contained in the database, which were readily apparent from cursory comparisons (Franceschini, Maisano, & Mastrogiacomo, 2016). Nonetheless, the Scopus interface makes it fairly simple to notify the company of any content problems that were encountered by users through a web form easily located on most Scopus pages. The support documentation for Scopus to this day demonstrates the relative simplicity of the process (Scopus, 2019). When Scopus first came on the market, Web of Science did not have a similar prominently identifiable means of submitting corrections. The corporate culture of Elsevier, which owns Scopus, is nonetheless a cause for concern among the research community (Swoger, 2013).

Scopus in the initial years opted to utilize metrics developed independently rather than internally, most notably SCImago Journal Rank (SJR) and Source Normalized Impact per Paper (SNIP). SJR, developed by the SCImago Group at the University of Extremadura in Spain seeks to measure a journal's "average prestige per paper" using weighted rankings and network analysis (González-Pereira, Guerrero-Bote, & Moya-Anegón, 2009, 3). The SJR is computed in a manner similar but not identical to Web of Science's Article Influence Score (AIS). Major differences include the size of the publication sets (relative to the size of the Scopus database versus that of Web of Science) the time frame from which citations are captured (three years for SJR and five years for AIS); and whether or not to include self-citations (SJR caps self-citation content, AIS excludes it entirely) (Davis, 2015).

The premise of SNIP, developed at the Center for Science and Technology Studies at Leiden University, was to create a metric that corrected for differing publication and citation rates between various disciplines. The means by which this was accomplished was to develop subject-based citation networks, establish citation frequency patterns within the network, then measure the citation rate of a publication against this "citation potential" as a probability calculation (Moed, 2010).

In June 2017, Scopus released CiteScore. At the simplest level, CiteScore is a journal's mean number of citations per publication. Dividing by number of publications corrects for the relative size of a journal; that is to say those journals which publish more articles do not automatically have a higher CiteScore. The calculation does not, however, correct for the persistent issue of varying disciplinary citation patterns and practices. To address this, Scopus added percentile rankings to contextualize a journal's CiteScore (James, Colledge, Meester, Azoulay, & Plume, 2018).

Google Scholar

Probably the most controversial citation data provider is Google Scholar, which, despite having no rhyme or reason to its coverage, gives often significantly higher citation counts than either of the proprietary tools. Several years ago, scholars estimated the size of Google Scholar at approximately 160–165 million records (Orduna-Malea, Ayllón, Martín-Martín, & Delgado López-Cózar, 2015). Many researchers favor the high citation counts despite concerns that Google Scholar is inadequate for bibliometric study and research evaluation (Halevi, Moed, & Bar-Ilan, 2017). A legitimate strength of Google

Scholar is that it covers more non-English language, non-First-World publications than either Scopus or Web of Science, as well as a tremendous amount of "gray" literature and scholarly output other than PRJAs (Haddaway, Collins, Coughlin, & Kirk, 2015; Martín-Martín, Orduna-Malea, Thelwall, & Delgado López-Cózar, 2018). In 2011, Google released an author profile tool called Google Scholar Citations, which provides author level metrics including their own *i-10 index*, simply the number of times cited in the past 10 years (Connor, 2011; Ortega & Aguillo, 2014).

h-Index

Aside from the indicators mentioned above, another well-known indicator for scientific achievement is the *h*-index. In his seminal work proposing the *h*-index as a measure of scholarly activity, Jorge Hirsch appears to complain that the common suite of citation-based metrics in vogue at the time (implicitly, those emanating from ISI/Web of Science), was a large amount of information for evaluators to digest and comprehend. Therefore, he devised an index that would provide a simplified metric for evaluative purposes (Hirsch, 2005). The *h*-index is meant to be used at the author level, but other units of research production are also sometimes measured. The simplest way to explain how to compute the *h*-index is to take the researcher's peer reviewed publications and rank them from highest to lowest number of times cited. Plot this ranking on a graph, with times cited on the *y*-axis, and label the ranked publication denoted as 1, 2, 3, so on across the *x*-axis. Then draw the line $x = y$. The integer where the number of times cited on the *y*-axis equals the number of papers on the *x*-axis is the researcher's *h*-index. Thus, *h*-index is a combination measure of productivity and impact, according to Hirsch. It is interesting to note that despite many concerns about using citation-based metrics for evaluation, Hirsch (2005) actually designed the *h*-index for the purpose of providing "a useful yardstick with which to compare, in an unbiased way, different individuals competing for the same resource when an important criterion is scientific achievement" (p. 16572). Gingras (2016), on the other hand, states that the *h*-index is essentially a useless metric, because it is an "arbitrary" composite of research quality and quantity, and that it smacks of the precept that "any number beats no number" (pp. 42–43). It may be the simplicity of the *h*-index that is so appealing to non-specialists. Reiterating the propensity to create metrics out of data that is easy to compile and analyze Gingras (2016) states:

> too many bibliometricians have focused exclusively on the intricacies of counting any units they could find (citations, tweets, views, web connections, etc.) instead of asking first: what is the meaning of these measures? (p. xi)

g-Index and Other *h*-Index Variations

Leo Egghe (2006) felt that Hirsch's indicator did not properly address what is usually a skewed distribution of citations to a scholar's oeuvre, therefore proposed a g-index where the "highest number of g papers that together received g^2 citations." The effect of squaring the citation count favors highly cited papers, and creates a more granular distinction between scholars' scores than does h-index. Egghe posits that this is of greater merit in distinguishing between the scholarly output or scientific achievement of various entities. In addition to Egghe's variation, many other alternatives have been made to the h-index to account for innumerable sorts of issues with one's scholarly career (Harzing, 2010). It is not readily discernible from anecdotal evidence of the practical application of scholarly metrics that Egghe's g-index or any of the other h-index variations appear to be widely adopted at this time. Web of Science, Scopus, and Google Scholar Citations all calculate an author's h-index. Because these citation indexing sources have differing publication coverage, a researcher's h-index can vary depending on which source is used.

Alternative (Alt)Metrics

With the advent of electronic publishing formats, increase in activity and recognition for good research spread across the World Wide Web on blogs, news sites, web pages, social media, and other places where researchers navigate to stay on top of current issues. Researchers sometimes access information from places they do not feel are valued for scholarly rigor, such as message boards, blogs, or the various online communities where researchers gather and share information. Thus, there is a tension between disciplinary standards and actual practice (Roemer & Borchardt, 2015b). Interest in a way to capture results of the sharing and dissemination of scholarly output in venues other than cited references in PRJAs started to gain momentum. For a good overview of the general merits and drawbacks of altmetrics, see Ann Williams' (2017) overview in *Online Information Review*.

Priem and Hemminger (2010) published one of the first papers in support of using scholarly metrics based on sources other than citations to PRJAs. In their opinion, merely capturing the citing references would no longer reflect whole domains of dissemination through social bookmarking, blogs, social media, and other content available on the Internet. They primarily direct the utility of these metrics at promotion and tenure and evaluation of researcher/scholar productivity in terms of not only research, but teaching and service as well. First considered "webometrics," there was an early recognition that the connections on the World Wide Web fostered a quick turnaround of knowledge dissemination. Priem and collaborators eventually refined this idea, dubbed these indicators "altmetrics" and generated the seminal work known as the *Altmetric manifesto*. The precise value of many altmetric indicators is not entirely recognized at this point; the manifesto explicitly states we need to "ask *how and why* as well as *how many*?" (Priem, Taraborelli, Groth, & Neylon, 2010). It is evident at the very least from the case studies in this book that altmetrics play a value in charting the path of dissemination of scholarly thought above and beyond researcher and disciplinary milieus.

Plum Analytics

A mere three years after Priem and his cohorts published their analysis and manifesto, Michael Buschman and Andrea Michalek published work on a similar theme. They identified five indicators of impact from non-peer reviewed journal sources: usage, captures, mentions, social media, and citations. These indicators remain the basis of the tool they created, PlumX and the visual display of their impact indicators known as the PlumPrint. They questioned, even at this early stage whether so-called alternative metrics were even still "alternative" (Buschman & Michalek, 2013). Since that time they have added significantly more content to their altmetric mix and can trace impact to a wide variety of scholarly outputs, not simply PRJAs (PlumX Metrics – Plum Analytics, n.d.). In 2014, Plum Analytics was acquired by Ebsco, and then later sold to Elsevier in 2017, which owns it to this day (Michalek, 2014, 2017). One author has likened Plum's metrics as a kind of "Nielsen Ratings" (Borofsky, 2012).

Altmetric.com

Euan Adie and his company were meanwhile yet another group creating an alternative metric tool of their own: Altmetric.com (Adie & Roe, 2013). Altmetric.com should not be confused with Priem et al.'s site: *altmetric.org*, although it is an easy error to commit. Adie and Roe described their main interest with Altmetric.com to be the collection of metadata about publication mentions and attention on the web and not developing a metric per se. Even still, the Altmetric "donut" and single-number Altmetric Attention Score appear to be an attempt at one cohesive indicator to integrate different sources such as: public policy documents, mainstream media, online reference managers, open peer review sources, Wikipedia, Open Syllabus Project, patents, blogs, citations, Faculty of 1000, social media, and multimedia (Altmetric, 2015).

Dimensions

In January 2018, Herzog and colleagues launched Dimensions, which may be the latest database or indexing innovation contributing to the study of the research process and of the evolution of scientific thought. The purpose of Dimensions is to bring together metadata about research through the entire process from grant to output. Therefore, in addition to including citation, patent, and altmetric data, Dimensions also includes resources on clinical trials, findings, and data sources related to research projects in various stages of the research cycle. Using linked data, it aims to be a system that helps the academic community to own the formulation and development of metrics that tell the best stories and give the best context to a piece of research. (Bode, Herzog, Hook, & McGrath, 2018)

Dimensions looks promising and its linked data model may show a more granular transmission of scholarly ideas and thought through the research process. Further, the ready connections to open access versions of publications render Dimensions a robust resource for research dissemination.

Becker Model

An interesting framework for measuring impact has come from the Bernard Becker Medical Library at Washington University at Saint Louis. Dubbed the Becker Model, it guides those looking to measure impact to map to real world changes that were made as a result of the research. Key areas for measurement are:

>Advancement of knowledge.
>Clinical implementation.
>Community benefit.
>Legislation and policy.
>Economic benefit (How to Use the Model, n.d.)

The Other Side of the Coin: Peer Review

Peer review, or the judgment of experts, is critical for the contextualization and understanding of research. But peer review itself can be less than optimal. Insular communities of scholars may be resistant to new ideas; studies show peer review can be random and subjective to a certain extent; and much like the incentives provided by scholarly metrics, the popular or attention-attracting topics get reviewed favorably, whereas obscure but innovative areas of research may be ignored or rejected (Cronin & Sugimoto, 2015, pp. 621–622). Despite its own limitations, peer review is a valuable tool for those who are not experts in the field to understand the relevance and significance of a given scholarly output to the greater discipline. For some, it remains preferable to any numeric metric (Cronin & Sugimoto, 2015, pp. 229–231). With open peer review and open access we may have a more public dialogue based not on blind peer review, which can be seen as removing reviewer accountability, but on all parties knowing full well their colleagues' agreement and disagreement with various theorems or research outputs. Open peer review models such as F1000, Kudos, and Publons may change the dynamic of peer review that we see above in new ways. As a result, measures of research impact and peer review remain counterpoints or checks and balances on the scholarly "rewards" system; both serve to provide differing contextual aspects about research output.

Gamesmanship and Fraud

In his book *The Tyranny of Metrics*, Muller (2018) points out that such measurements are a form of surveillance and that reliance on indicators to measure scholarly performance may create collateral behaviors which do not incentivize innovation or new lines of inquiry. Evaluators' reliance on research impact metrics has lent at least some validation to concerns of gamesmanship. For example, the *Journal of Criminal Justice* (*JCJ*), indexed by Web of Science, saw a dramatic leap in its JIF score when the editor undertook an extensive practice of increasing the citation count of *JCJ*. He did this by publishing a large number of articles that cited *JCJ*, the vast majority of which he authored himself (Bartlett, 2015).

Through the years there has also been evidence of citation "cartels" where networks of scholars or journals essentially conspire to increase citations to each other in order for improved citation metrics across the network/cartel (Fister, Fister, & Perc, 2016). Certainly, if the JIF and other citation metrics did not hold very significant weight among a variety of stakeholders, the somewhat laborious undertakings such gamesmanship requires would not be worth the effort.

Nonetheless, gamesmanship or fraud, while egregious, are not the most common cause of research impact metric misuse. Administrators, campus committees, and those evaluators of research projects not intimately familiar with the standards and/or cultural norms of a given discipline can be inclined to view a score as a kind of summarizing shorthand that allows them to quantify the context provided by more narrative materials; for example, in the case of academia: a promotion or tenure candidate's letters of external review, his or her teaching and service oeuvre, and other items listed on his or her curriculum vita. Reliance on metrics to supplant or simplify the evaluative process can be subtle or not so subtle, but it is a form of misuse that harms both the research entity and the evaluative entity. A glaringly common example of this type of misuse is the propensity to apply journal-level metrics to measure individuals or other units of researcher collaboration. Despite being well documented as inappropriate, scientists felt compelled to formulate a Declaration on Research Assessment for scholars, researchers, and institutions to sign in an effort to spread knowledge and understanding about the misuse and misinterpretation of various research impact indicators, particularly the use of JIF as a measure of researcher achievement (Paulus, Cruz, & Krach, 2018; San Francisco Declaration on Research Assessment (DORA), 2019).

Surprisingly, fraud and gamesmanship in altmetrics do not seem to be a greater threat to metric integrity than in citation-based metrics. Fraud for this type of metrics usually centers around the automated creation of fake profiles or sites, known as "bots." Due to their automated nature, bots are thus far able to be spotted and filtered from most altmetric tools (Haustein et al., 2016; Liu & Adie, 2013; Roemer & Borchardt, 2015a). It may be worthwhile to note that similar concerns have been voiced about the creation of fake publications on Google Scholar (Delgado López-Cózar, Robinson-García, & Torres-Salinas, 2014). While it may be simple to automate fraud for these purposes, it is also possible to automate the filtering of bots as well, much like unwanted emails or "spam." Like spam filters, bot filters are effective, so long as the computer programmers remain vigilant.

The Spread of Scholarly Metrics in Specialized Settings

Although they have been long-used in colleges and universities, the use of research impact metrics is increasingly persistent in more specialized settings, and for reasons other than, or perhaps in addition to, the career trajectory of researchers and scientists.

The case studies you see here represent five examples of such specialization. The domains of physical sciences, social sciences, and humanities are all touched upon. While two of the cases are directly affiliated with single institutions of higher learning (University of Michigan Press and UC Berkeley's Institute for Transportation Studies), these cases do not represent typical academic disciplinary departments with the usual academic needs and concerns. In all cases, it is the staff of the organization's internal information centers, classified as *special libraries,* that provide these services to their parent organizations (instead of "special," the term "specialized" is perhaps more descriptive and self-evident outside of the library community). Not all the staff who compile and provide this information possess library science degrees, however. Libraries and information centers are uniquely suited to providing impact metrics services as well as instructing stakeholders and constituencies on the strengths, limitations, and appropriate use of such indicators. This is true for a number of reasons. For example, libraries have expertise in using bibliometrics to evaluate library materials for collection retention and acquisition policies. Libraries are cross-disciplinary and generally serve all constituencies across an organization. To take that point further, libraries have no "horse in the race;" Generally they represent neutral entities in the provision of the information to the various stakeholders who need to demonstrate the impact of a body of research in order to further organizational mission and vision.

The Case Studies

Briefly, here is an overview of the cases presented in this book. Each provides insight into the breadth and depth of how research impact can be tracked, measured, and communicated to stakeholders.

National Center for Atmospheric Research (NCAR): NCAR is doing very interesting and labor-intensive work related to measuring the scholarly output of associated researchers, the use of a supercomputer, as well as the EarthCube infrastructure. NCAR's library has excelled through incorporation of home-built applications and implementation of technology solutions to obtain and analyze important data about impact and reach.

University of Michigan Press (UMP): With access to an impressive suite of bibliometric, altmetric, and data analytics tools, UMP leverages information about its monographs, journals, and unique repository items to make informed decisions about the viability of open access and community-supported publishing models. UMP also seeks to get its publications indexed in the right sources to assure they will be discoverable, and therefore citable.

Institute for Transportation Studies (ITS) at UC Berkeley: Answerable ultimately to the California State Legislature, ITS at UC Berkeley has laid the foundation for tracking the dissemination and reach of multidisciplinary transportation-related projects, technical reports, and other gray literature using manual indexing and Google Scholar data, as well as other low- or no-cost sources.

United States Environmental Protection Agency (EPA): Librarians at the EPA have leveled up in their ability to create and replicate visually eye-catching reports and infographics that provide stakeholders with vital information about the reach and success of scholarly activity and its applications in enforcing environmental policy and regulations.

Natural History Museum: A proof-of-concept demonstrating the value of altmetrics tools for a humanities and social sciences museum shows that the information provided can help a museum tailor its programming for online and in-person programming, justify research expenses to donors, and complement public relations and other information in providing an understanding of the museum's overall reach and impact in a variety of sectors.

These case studies will be of primary use to a research organization's subunit, usually the library or information center, that seeks to provide or improve the provision of research impact services. Internal to the organization, high-level administrators, researchers/scientists, and associated staff may find this work helpful in understanding what is possible for their organization and its information center, if given the time, opportunity, and resources. Externally all stripes of research evaluators, whether funders/donors, policymakers, or others who wish to understand the value in an organization's research output, will gain a better understanding of what information could be used in assessment. This may in turn help evaluators better communicate what impact measures and other scientometric data will effectively demonstrate success or achievement on the part of the organization. The projects described in this work will hopefully provide inspiration and food for thought at what will best work in a variety of specialized settings.

References

Adie, E., & Roe, W. (2013). Altmetric: Enriching scholarly content with article-level discussion and metrics. *Learned Publishing*, *26*(1), 11–17. DOI:10.1087/20130103

Altmetric. (2015, July 9). Our sources. https://www.altmetric.com/about-our-data/our-sources/.

American Association for the Advancement of Science. (2018, April). Historical trends in Federal R&D. https://www.aaas.org/programs/r-d-budget-and-policy/historical-trends-federal-rd.

Bartlett, T. (2015). The journal that couldn't stop citing itself. *The Chronicle of Higher Education*, September 23. https://www.chronicle.com/article/The-Journal-That-Couldnt-Stop/233313.

Bergstrom, C. (2007). Eigenfactor: Measuring the value and prestige of scholarly journals. *College & Research Libraries News*, *68*(5), 314–316.

Bode, C., Herzog, C., Hook, D., & McGrath, R. (2018). A guide to the Dimensions data approach. *A collaborative approach to creating a modern infrastructure for data describing research: Where we are and where we want to take it*. London: Digital Science. https://www.digital-science.com/resources/portfolio-reports/a-guide-to-the-dimensions-data-approach/.

Borofsky, Y. (2012, March 14). Plum analytics: "kind of like Nielson ratings" for academic research launches Alpha. https://technical.ly/philly/2012/03/14/plum-analytics-kind-of-like-nielson-ratings-for-academic-research-launches-alpha/.

Buschman, M., & Michalek, A. (2013). Are alternative metrics still alternative? *Bulletin of the American Society for Information Science and Technology*, *39*(4), 35–39. DOI:10.1002/bult.2013.1720390411

Clarivate Analytics. (2017). *Web of science fact book* (pp. 1–4). https://clarivate.com/wp-content/uploads/2017/05/d6b7faae-3cc2-4186-8985-a6ecc8cce1ee_Crv_WoS_Upsell_Factbook_A4_FA_LR_edits.pdf

Connor, J. (2011, July 20). Google scholar citations. https://scholar.googleblog.com/2011/07/google-scholar-citations.html.

Cronin, B., & Sugimoto, C. R. (Eds.). (2015). *Scholarly metrics under the microscope: From citation analysis to academic auditing*. Medford, NJ: Published on behalf of the Association for Information Science and Technology by Information Today, Inc.

Davis, P. (2015, July 28). Network-based citation metrics: Eigenfactor vs. SJR. https://scholarlykitchen.sspnet.org/2015/07/28/network-based-citation-metrics-eigenfactor-vs-sjr/.

Delgado López-Cózar, E., Robinson-García, N., & Torres-Salinas, D. (2014). The Google scholar experiment: How to index false papers and manipulate bibliometric indicators: Journal of the American Society for Information Science and Technology. *Journal of the Association for Information Science and Technology*, 65(3), 446–454. DOI:10.1002/asi.23056

Egghe, L. (2006). An improvement of the *h*-index: The *g*-index. *ISSI Newsletter*, 2(1), 8–9.

Fister, I. J., Fister, I., & Perc, M. (2016). Toward the discovery of citation Cartels in citation networks. *Frontiers in Physics*, 4. DOI:10.3389/fphy.2016.00049

Franceschini, F., Maisano, D., & Mastrogiacomo, L. (2016). The museum of errors/horrors in Scopus. *Journal of Informetrics*, 10(1), 174–182. DOI:10.1016/j.joi.2015.11.006

Gingras, Y. (2016). *Bibliometrics and research evaluation: uses and abuses*. Cambridge, MA: The MIT Press.

González-Pereiraa, B., Guerrero-Boteb, V. P., & Moya-Anegónc, F. (2009). The SJR indicator: A new indicator of journals' scientific prestige. *ArXiv Preprint ArXiv:0912.4141*.

Haddaway, N. R., Collins, A. M., Coughlin, D., & Kirk, S. (2015). The Role of Google Scholar in Evidence Reviews and Its Applicability to Grey Literature Searching. *PLOS ONE*, 10(9), e0138237. DOI:10.1371/journal.pone.0138237

Halevi, G., Moed, H., & Bar-Ilan, J. (2017). Suitability of Google Scholar as a source of scientific information and as a source of data for scientific evaluation—Review of the Literature. *Journal of Informetrics*, 11(3), 823–834. DOI:10.1016/j.joi.2017.06.005

Harzing, A.-W. (2010). *The publish or perish book: Your guide to effective and responsible citation analysis* (1st ed.). Melbourne, Australia: Tarma Software Research.

Haustein, S., Bowman, T. D., Holmberg, K., Tsou, A., Sugimoto, C. R., & Larivière, V. (2016). Tweets as impact indicators: Examining the implications of automated "bot" accounts on Twitter. *Journal of the Association for Information Science and Technology*, 67(1), 232–238. DOI:10.1002/asi.23456

Hirsch, J. E. (2005). An index to quantify an individual's scientific research output. *Proceedings of the National Academy of Sciences of the United States of America*, 102(46), 16569–16572. DOI:10.1073/pnas.0507655102

Institute of Medicine. (2004). *Immunization Safety Review: Vaccines and Autism*. DOI:10.17226/10997

James, C., Colledge, L., Meester, W., Azoulay, N., & Plume, A. (2018). CiteScore metrics: Creating journal metrics from the Scopus citation index, 16. https://arxiv.org/ftp/arxiv/papers/1812/1812.06871.pdf

Lawler, B. (2014). The Institute for Scientific Information: A brief history. In L. R. McEwen & R. E. Buntrock (Eds.), *The future of the history of chemical information* (pp. 109–126). Washington, DC: American Chemical Society.

Liu, J., & Adie, E. (2013). Five challenges in altmetrics: A toolmaker's perspective. *Bulletin of the American Society for Information Science and Technology*, 39(4), 31–34. DOI:10.1002/bult.2013.1720390410

Martín-Martín, A., Orduna-Malea, E., Thelwall, M., & Delgado López-Cózar, E. (2018). Google Scholar, Web of Science, and Scopus: A systematic comparison of citations in 252 subject categories. *Journal of Informetrics*, 12(4), 1160–1177. DOI:10.1016/j.joi.2018.09.002

A Brief History and Overview 13

Michalek, A. (2014, January 15). Plum analytics becomes part of EBSCO information services – Plum Analytics [Blog]. https://plumanalytics.com/plum-analytics-becomes-part-of-ebsco-information-services/.

Michalek, A. (2017, February 2). Plum analytics joins Elsevier – Plum analytics [Blog]. https://plumanalytics.com/plum-analytics-joins-elsevier/.

Moed, H. F. (2010). Measuring contextual citation impact of scientific journals. *Journal of Informetrics, 4*(3), 265–277. DOI:10.1016/j.joi.2010.01.002

Muller, J. Z. (2018). *The tyranny of metrics.* Princeton, NJ: Princeton University Press.

Nowakowska, M. (1990). Cluster analysis, graphs, and branching processes as new methodologies for intelligent systems on example of bibliometric and social network data. *International Journal of Intelligent Systems, 5*(3), 247–263. DOI:10.1002/int.4550050303

Orduna-Malea, E., Ayllón, J. M., Martín-Martín, A., & Delgado López-Cózar, E. (2015). Methods for estimating the size of Google Scholar. *Scientometrics, 104*(3), 931–949. DOI:10.1007/s11192-015-1614-6

Ortega, J. L., & Aguillo, I. F. (2014). Microsoft academic search and Google scholar citations: Comparative analysis of author profiles. *Journal of the Association for Information Science and Technology, 65*(6), 1149–1156. DOI:10.1002/asi.23036

Paulus, F. M., Cruz, N., & Krach, S. (2018). The impact factor Fallacy. *Frontiers in Psychology, 9*, 1487. DOI:10.3389/fpsyg.2018.01487

PlumX Metrics - Plum Analytics. (n.d.). Retrieved February 3, 2019, from https://plumanalytics.com/learn/about-metrics/

Priem, J., & Hemminger, B. H. (2010). Scientometrics 2.0: New metrics of scholarly impact on the social Web. *First Monday, 15*(7). http://pear.accc.uic.edu/ojs/index.php/fm/article/viewArticle/2874

Priem, J., Taraborelli, D., Groth, P., & Neylon, C. (2010, October 26). *Altmetrics: a manifesto.* Retrieved January 18, 2019, from Altmetrics.org website: http://altmetrics.org/manifesto/

Pritchard, A. (1969). Statistical bibliography or bibliometrics. *Journal of Documentation, 25*(4), 348–349.

Ritter, S. K. (2003). Science, Religion, and the Art of Cold Fusion. *Chemical & Engineering News, 81*(34), 33–33. DOI:10.1021/cen-v081n034.p033

Raan, T. (2014). Advances in bibliometric analysis: Research performance assessment and science mapping. In Blockmans, W., et al., (Eds.), *Bibliometrics, Use and Abuse in the Review of Research Performance.* London: Portland Press, Ltd.

Roemer, R. C., & Borchardt, R. (2015a). Issues, controversies, and opportunities for altmetrics. *Library Technology Reports, 51*(5), 20–30.

Roemer, R. C., & Borchardt, R. (Eds.). (2015b). *Meaningful metrics: A 21st century librarian's guide to bibliometrics, altmetrics, and research impact.* Chicago, IL: Association of College and Research Libraries, a division of the American Library Association.

San Francisco Declaration on Research Assessment (DORA). (2019, January 18). https://sfdora.org/.

Scopus. (2019). Profile and content corrections support center. https://service.elsevier.com/app/home/supporthub/scopuscontent/.

Stevenson, A. (2010). *Pure science.* http://www.oxfordreference.com/view/10.1093/acref/9780199571123.001.0001/m_en_gb0674580

Swoger, B. (2013, December 12). Is Elsevier really for-science? Or just for-profit? Retrieved January 30, 2019, from Scientific American Blog Network website: https://blogs.scientificamerican.com/information-culture/is-elsevier-really-for-science-or-just-for-profit/

Williams, A. E. (2017). Altmetrics: An overview and evaluation. *Online Information Review, 41*(3), 311–317. DOI:10.1108/OIR-10-2016-0294

Wilsdon, J., Allen, L., Belfiore, E., Campbell, P., Curry, S., Hill, S., ... Johnson, B. (2015). *The metric tide: Report of the independent review of the role of metrics in research assessment and management.* Unpublished. DOI:10.13140/rg.2.1.4929.1363

Chapter 2

Scholarly Metrics at NCAR

Keith Maull and Matthew Mayernik

Overview

The National Center for Atmospheric Research (NCAR) is a National Science Foundation (NSF)-funded research laboratory whose mission is to:

> understand the behavior of the atmosphere and related Earth and geospace systems; to support, enhance, and extend the capabilities of the university community and the broader scientific community, nationally and internationally; and to foster the transfer of knowledge and technology for the betterment of life on Earth.

As an R&D laboratory, NCAR produces hundreds of peer-reviewed publications annually, and there is vigorous interest in understanding those publications against the landscape of scholarly contribution to their respective fields. The NCAR Library in collaboration with other management entities at the organization has led efforts to develop scholarly metrics to track, visualize, and explore the publication record of the organization. This chapter will describe the scholarly metrics efforts at NCAR, with focus on the origins, objectives, and outcomes of institutional scholarly metrics as well as its future goals.

Introduction

Large research organizations such as universities and laboratories have a vested interest in tracking the research activities of their communities. Many of these research activities culminate *formally* as scholarly publications, in journals, conference proceedings, articles, and books, and are often measured. Metrics for these types of research outputs are most often captured by *bibliometrics*, and today many publishers provide platforms (e.g., Web of Science and Scopus) for organizational views of such metrics so that a variety of data may be tracked, such as cumulative citations, the scope and span of research topics, the breadth and diversity of collaborations (both peer and institutional), the perceived quality of the venues in which such publications appear, and so on. Built atop bibliometrics, but more broadly focused on the socio-digital footprints of publications, *alternative metrics* (or "altmetrics") aim at exposing the informal and social media attention that scholarship often now receive (Piwowar, 2013). Different in approach than traditional bibliometrics, altmetrics simply provide another tool to measure and predict the impact of scholarly work. Though there are many debates on the value, completeness, accuracy, and robustness of these formal and informal metrics (Costas, Zahedi, & Wouters, 2015; Haustein, 2016), together, and with other relevant and focused data, they help paint a more robust picture of the research activities of an organization.

Historically, information scientists have been the purveyors of scholarly metrics. Citation analysis was developed as a legitimate method for studying the dynamics and productivity of scholars in the 1960s, alongside the emergence of broadly accessible tools and databases (Garfield, 1979). The broader fields of bibliometrics and informetrics evolved considerably over the subsequent decades to encompass many kinds of scholarly resources and evaluation methods (Borgman & Furner, 2002; Milojević & Leydesdorff, 2013). Today, scholarly metrics are used in a variety of ways, from assessing the complete body of work of an individual scholar for promotion and awards to building complex tools to demonstrate and report scholarly impact to funding agencies and prospective collaborators (Ilik et al., 2018; Moed, 2005). Increasingly, these metrics are used to make important organizational decisions that draw from many sources, and libraries have become the central force behind many scholarly metrics efforts (Gutzman et al., 2018). Libraries have historically been seen as the responsible, trusted and neutral intercessor of information and data, making them ideally situated to understand the nuanced implications of various indicators while leaving domain experts to contextualize metrics within their own fields.

This chapter presents scholarly metrics initiatives within the NCAR Library. NCAR is an NSF-funded federally funded research and development center, with the mission of conducting fundamental scientific research into atmospheric, solar, and geophysical phenomenon. The management of NCAR research and resources is directed by the University Corporation for Atmospheric Research (UCAR) on behalf of the NSF and in concert with nearly 115 degree-granting North American member universities with geoscience programs. UCAR provides support and services to promote research, education, and resource sharing with and among member universities and NCAR. The activities of NCAR and its university community partners are therefore important to track and understand, as such activities help guide decision-making about future collaborations, resource allocations, and program development. Though varied in scope, scholarly activities that yield outcomes such as publications are of particular interest since they can be easily tracked, quantified, and analyzed.

At NCAR, the Library has the stated high-level mission of "providing services and systems that promote discovery, preserve knowledge, and improve scholarly communication," and scholarly metrics have now become an important part of the ongoing development of that mission. NCAR scientists produce hundreds of scholarly publications annually, and NCAR member faculty and researchers many hundreds more.

Metrics at NCAR Library

Since the inception of NCAR, there have been reporting directives from the NSF that culminate in an annual report now called the "NCAR Annual Report" or NAR. The NAR summarizes the activities of NCAR over the reporting period, including significant research achievements, specific management activities, service and scientific accomplishments of staff, and the alignment of these activities with the strategic goals of the institution. Also included in the NAR is a comprehensive bibliography of NCAR staff authored and co-authored peer-reviewed publications. Over the lifetime of the NAR, the NCAR Library has been both the curator and the custodian of this bibliography. These yearly bibliographies represent the most complete public record of research activity of the institution and have been used as important indicators of the scientific impact of the organization. Until recently, however, they were primarily used to detail individual or group-level accomplishments. For example, a specific publication written by an NCAR science team might be used to show how the research contributions of a coordinated group of authors had expanded the scientific understanding of the phenomenon under study. However, for most of the NAR's past, comprehensive citation counts of publications were largely unknown – scientists "knew" the impact of a paper due to their own citing behavior and that of others. As the need to develop a standardized concept of publication "impact," citation counts, h-indices and journal impact factors became sought after metrics, because they are key metrics of focus within bibliometrics research.

The NCAR Library's involvement in the development of the NAR bibliography is extensive. Historically, all NCAR personnel were asked to self-report information about all of their publication and service activities – which importantly includes peer-reviewed publications. NCAR Library staff would take these self-reported peer-reviewed publications and cross-validate them against similar information provided by key administrative and management personnel in each research laboratory. These two data sources were then collated against one another and finalized. The final NAR bibliography is then published as the definitive record of peer-reviewed scholarship for that year's research activity.

These activities are time consuming and require many hours of staff effort, and as NAR bibliographies expanded, the need for automation became apparent, but so did the need for a strategy to apply and standardize metrics over the entire body of NCAR peer-reviewed scholarship these bibliographies represented. In 2013, the Library began subscribing to the Clarivate Analytics (formerly Thomson Reuters) Web of Science *InCites* product. *InCites* uses standardized institutional affiliations to automatically scan the many thousands of peer-reviewed publisher databases for publications attributable to NCAR. *InCites* provided accurate, up-to-date and detailed institutional publication information, and it was quickly integrated into the NCAR Library NAR bibliography research process as yet another tool to derive the complete publication and research activities of the institution. By using *automated filters* to generate an annual bibliography within Web of Science specifically tailored to NCAR publications (tuned for disambiguated author-organization references), the human effort is reduced to NCAR Library staff verifying accuracy and correctness before publishing as the definitive annual NAR bibliography. The publications (or preprints depending on publisher agreements) are then made available within NCAR's online open repository, OpenSky (https://opensky.ucar.edu), which is managed and maintained by the Library.

The increase of highly detailed machine-readable publication metadata and corresponding computational techniques for analyzing that metadata, correlated with increased interest in more detailed analysis of the data captured by this bibliography. For example, along with complete bibliographies, corresponding citation metrics were desired. These citation metrics were the gateway to more sophisticated metrics, for example, detailing the collaboration networks of NCAR authors to provide insights into *whom* they were working with and *how much*; deepening the understanding of *non-human resources* used in the production of publication outcomes (such as instruments, computational facilities, software, etc.); or understanding the funding mix of various research activities within the organization. Such metrics lend themselves to more comprehensive views of scholarly impact that contextualize the many components of scholarly publications.

The NCAR Library thus began a focused effort on using and developing tools and platforms to support a variety of traditional and new analyses. For example, citation counts alone do not provide a complete picture of the "importance" of a publication, and further still the "quality" that citation counts imply about a publication remains the topic of widespread and vigorous discussion (Nicolaisen, 2007; Tahamtan & Bornmann, 2018). Any metrics-based analysis faces challenges of interpretation, namely, how to understand what the metrics mean in the context of particular evaluation questions (Tague, 1988). Similarly, other questions are necessary when trying to understand how a publication came to produce an important outcome. For example, the resources used in the production of an important publication, that is, the instruments, computational platforms, software, etc. must be critically considered, since the outcomes of the publication may not have been possible without them.

NCAR Library Metrics Case Studies

As detailed in the previous section, UCAR manages and coordinates the activities of NCAR through the broad network of degree-granting member universities that are represented in many of the collaborative research activities of NCAR. Since the vast majority of NCAR's funding support is through the NSF, we will detail three case studies where metrics were used in very different ways to support the goals and interests of those requesting them.

NCAR Supercomputer Community Metrics and Lessons Learned

Since the 1960s, NCAR has operated and managed a world-class supercomputing infrastructure focused primarily on high-performance computing for geoscience and atmospheric modeling problems. Funded by the NSF, this infrastructure supports a variety of research computing activities through high-performance petaflop-scale computing, high-speed petabyte on-demand storage, and over a quarter-exabyte archival storage. At least half of the active users of the supercomputer are atmospheric science researchers at, or affiliated with, a UCAR member university, while the remainder is NCAR scientists performing a breadth of research computing tasks. Operating the supercomputer is thus an essential function of NCAR, and the primary source of funding for the resource comes from the NSF.

Since the supercomputer is considered a "community" resource, its users and uses are varied, and while most of the jobs it serves are for atmospheric modeling research, the outcomes of that research are difficult to track. Accounts given to users do require details about the purpose of the account, the kinds of resources required of the account, as well as estimated duration of account activity. Additional details are also captured, such as the research program, funding agencies and NSF grant award numbers, and identifier(s) associated with the account. This account information is important data that are tracked and reported to funders, but only until recently did an interest develop in connecting these data with deeper scholarly metrics.

As mentioned previously, the *primary* function of the supercomputer is for research, and while not all research produces scholarly publications, scholarly publications are considered the culminating product of research. Thus, in 2009, the Computational Information Systems Laboratory (CISL) supercomputer group began administering an annual survey to all users of the supercomputer, which asked a number of questions about publications and other products (software, data, posters, etc.) that were produced as a result of their supercomputer use. This survey served two functions. First, it gave CISL a way to understand the publications that were associated with the supercomputer, since (informal and formal) citing and acknowledging behaviors of authors are inconsistent and unreliable; and second, it provided a way to report back to the NSF how the resource was important in the production of scholarly output. After several years of collecting this information, the obvious next step was to develop a broader context for the publications themselves. Knowing *which* publications utilized the supercomputer was a gateway to broader questions about the bibliometric profiles of those publications; for example, how many citations they had accumulated, which journals were popular for them to appear in, their authorship and institutional profiles, among other inquiries over the aggregate data.

Around the time of CISL's interest in expanded bibliometric analyses of user publications, the NCAR Library was working on an initial service offering of metrics aimed at asking many of the questions being asked by CISL. The NCAR Library first began working with the raw data from the surveys to develop an initial understanding of the underlying data. This initial data preprocessing required parsing the raw survey files for citations, which were provided by respondents as free text. Where DOIs were provided in the citation, they were used as the identifier for the citation. Where DOIs were missing, each citation was looked up and matching DOIs were then associated with the corresponding citation. Using DOIs for identifying the scholarly work provided a way to standardize the identifier, but also it expedited metadata extraction since the tools that were used to gather the full metrics profile of the publications required DOIs. It should be noted that publications that did not have a DOI or where a DOI could not be found were dropped from analysis. These publications represented less than 10% of all the publications reported.

Once the complete set of identifiers was extracted, the Library's bibliometrics services were put to full use. As part of the initial service offering, basic bibliometric information such as citation count, journal information, author names, and institutional affiliations were collected and analyzed. Since there were thousands of corresponding data points over all identifiers, the Library developed an initial automation workflow on top of a custom-built Application Programing Interface (API), which was developed to aggregate data and facilitate access from various data providers such as Crossref and Thomson Reuters Web of Science (now Clarivate Analytics Web of Science). The API also provided direct access to metrics data over the CISL collection so that aggregate and drill-down analyses could be performed.

NCAR Supercomputer Metrics Outcomes. The supercomputer metrics were the first meaningful test of the Library's metrics capabilities on real data. There were several aspects of the data that made the analysis unique. First, the publications were self-reported and even though the mean response rate was 25%, this is considered an exceptionally high rate. This response rate also proved a sufficiently strong estimator of the actual number of papers using the supercomputer (Hart, Rishel, & Nychka, 2016) and from the self-reported data, there were 803 total publications over the five-year period from 2008 to 2013. Those publications accumulated 13,007 citations for a publication set citations per publication rate of 16.2. Interestingly, the supercomputer was upgraded from the Bluefire supercomputer to the Yellowstone platform during the 2012 survey year. This did not materially change any of the outcomes. Second, the publications were centered on and traceable to a computational platform infrastructure (e.g., supercomputer). This is novel because tracing computationally intensive publications back to the source platform requires the authors appropriately acknowledge the resource or cite the persistent identifier of the platform, if one exists. Finally, the metrics confirmed but also expanded CISL's understanding of the measurable outputs of the community. For example, the metrics were able to show which institutions had the most lead (first) authors – the University of Colorado or University of Washington with 44 and 34 lead first author publications, respectively. The metrics also showed the most cited papers *not* led by NCAR authors. This was valuable in demonstrating that while the supercomputer is hosted by NCAR, and that NCAR scientists have access to, and significantly use the resource for their own research, that many highly cited publications were led by non-NCAR institutions. For example, the most cited non-NCAR author-led publication lead by an author from the University of Maryland accumulated 420 citations at the time of the metrics analysis.

Invariably, questions arise about the subject areas of the publications produced. The metrics uncovered that over 44 subject areas were covered by the 803 publications and that they were unsurprisingly dominated by meteorology, atmospheric science, geoscience (general), oceanography, astronomy, astrophysics, and environmental sciences. Additionally, fluids and plasma physics along with mechanics and computer science were substantially represented, confirming what many operating the facility already knew: the supercomputer was heavily used for complex fluid dynamic (atmospheric) simulation and high-performance computing research, which require supercomputer environments that have the necessary processing power, storage, and tool support to conduct such research.

There were not any reporting requirements for metrics display, so the Library recommended a single-page summary of a variety of metrics. The full one-page summary is shown in the Appendix. An experimental aspect of the summary that added visual interest to the report was a rudimentary word-cloud over the high-frequency words extracted from all included publication abstracts. Even though the word cloud did not transmit precise metrics, it drew attention to the broad thematic research topics that emerged from the publications. For example, it is very clear from the word cloud that modeling, simulation, and precipitation were common research themes.

NSF Site Visit Team Metrics

After the success of the supercomputer metrics, other groups began collaborating with the Library for smaller metrics analyses. The next significant utilization of the services came in 2016, when the NSF performed a series of comprehensive site visits to NCAR. Over the course of four months, various site visit teams (SVTs) came to NCAR to review the management and performance outcomes of NCAR laboratories, facilities, and personnel. Presentations were an integral part of each multi-day review, and the Library was asked to develop metrics that would be presented as part of the accomplishment profile of the organization.

Each site visit was thematically focused into three primary areas corresponding to the key activities of NCAR: (1) modeling, (2) observation, and (3) computation. As part of each review, metrics were presented to provide a profile of each activity and in order to adapt to the specialized demands of each area, the Library formalized, then adapted the workflow built from the initial work done with the supercomputer-user publication analysis. The adaptations were required to address a broadened scale and scope. The supercomputer-related publications numbered fewer than 1,000 and addressed a limited community, while the site visit theme publications spanned nearly a decade and numbered each in the several thousands.

NCAR management set an aggressive timeline for the SVT metrics requests and the Library was asked to develop standardized publications metrics profile reports for each thematic area within a matter of a few weeks, thus the planning phase of the workflow process was significantly abbreviated. Two Library staff were assigned with metrics extraction and analysis tasks, while several experts from NCAR research groups and laboratories associated with each thematic area were assigned with collecting relevant publications related to the research within that theme. The hard criterion for inclusion was that either the publication included an NCAR-affiliated author or the publication cited (or otherwise referred to) an NCAR-managed resource (e.g., computational model, software, supercomputing platform, etc.). Much of this work had already been done, as many groups within NCAR routinely collected such publication lists to develop a broad understanding of the communities they serve, as well as to keep internal metrics of their own publication productivity. However, a lot of additional work was necessary to compile these lists; for example, some of the lists did not include the most current research literature. This situation required significant literature searches to compile the most current and up-to-date publications.

This collection, management, and organization process imposed dramatically different requirements from the work previously done with the supercomputer group. First, the scale was much broader than before, but more importantly, the collaborative nature of the data collection process required that publication sets be simultaneously updated – there were several curators simultaneously revising and adding publications. (A *publication set* is a collection of publications, not unlike a bibliography, that may be unformatted, unstructured, and in the case most often used in this work, simply be a large set of DOIs that reference underlying publications.) Furthermore, the condensed timeline required a streamlined process, thus each thematic publication team chose to manage their lists as standard text files within Google Sheets. Each line in a document contained a single DOI representing a theme-relevant publication as required by the inclusion criteria. In cases where there were multiple files for a single research area (e.g., modeling), each file was merged into a single de-duplicated master file before analysis. This simplified, semi-formal approach, permitted work to be performed asynchronously, yet collaboratively by both the Library staff and each thematic team. The Library staff provided support where necessary, but more importantly had freedom to focus on critical metrics and analytics tasks.

The collection process took a couple of weeks and went more smoothly than anticipated. The simplified shared document approach to editing accelerated data entry and since de-duplication was a post-processing step, there was no pressure to verify that a DOI had already been entered into a document. And while documents got very large this did not slow progress in any meaningful way. In all, just under 8,000 unique DOIs were extracted for the "observation" and "modeling" theme documents, and the "computation" theme largely drew from the supercomputer work previously done – only a few new publications were added to the analysis that had already been performed. Table 1 shows details of each analysis area, the number of publications, and brief high-level statistics for each.

As can be seen, the scope and scale of the publication metrics varied widely between analyses, and this was a result of several factors. First, because the analyses were grouped into broad research areas, this meant that multiple research divisions within NCAR were grouped into a single research area. This meant that the coordination of publication sets between these groups varied widely. Not only did this affect the publication collection and management strategy, but it also required compiling publications from several independent data collectors. The Library simplified this process by allowing each group to compile and manage

Table 1: High-level metrics profile showing the SVT areas: Modeling, observation, and computing

	Modeling	Observation	Computing
Total citations	72,453	105,076	18,193
Cites/pub	25.140	20.919	19.437
Expected cites/pub[a]	13.6	13.6	13.6
Unique institutions	1,651	2,110	670
Unique authors	7,106	8,904	2,221
Authors/pub	8.096	6.207	5.391

[a](2005–2015) for Meteorology & Atmospheric Sciences (Clarivate Web of Science).

their own publication list (of DOIs) as a Google document to facilitate rapid collaboration and integration. Second, the time scales of each analysis varied in terms of their scientific impact. For example, the "computation" analysis only included publications between 2008 and 2015, whereas the "modeling" analysis included publications from 2005 through 2015. The additional three years of publications not only increased the total number of publications, but also the time for citations to accumulate, thus increasing the aggregate citation counts and ultimate impact of the publication metrics. Finally, the composition of the groups and organizational configurations over the course of each analysis differed in important ways. Since each analysis did not engage a single NCAR group or division, the variance between analyses was obvious; the boundaries between groups under a single analysis theme, the research each were performing, the number of scientists and research personnel in each group, the disciplinary collaborations, unexpected (and planned) organizational expansion, and contraction, among other factors, contributed to the size, breadth, and depth of the metrics that culminated in the high-level SVT reports about the scientific publications produced at NCAR.

The finalized metrics for each thematic unit included the following: the timespan of each publication analysis, the total number of publications included in each thematic analysis, total citations and average citations per publication, expected citations for Meteorology and Atmospheric Sciences (extracted from Web of Science data), total unique institutions, total unique authors, in addition to average authors per publication. Additionally, metrics included detailed affiliation information of authors, but specifically the number of publications where all, some, or none of the authors cited their primary affiliation as NCAR. This is an important approximation of the collaborative activities of NCAR, which exists in large part to stimulate and foster research collaborations. For example, one of the primary activities of NCAR is to *develop tools and resources* for the atmospheric community at large. Collaborations around such tools often do not involve *co-authorship* of publications, and thus are more appropriately measured by *resource utilization and citation* (e.g., using or citing NCAR developed models, techniques, and data) (Mayernik, Hart, Maull, & Weber, 2017). The metrics in the SVT reports overwhelmingly demonstrated this. Across the three thematic units, which included over 8,800 publications between 2005 and 2015, only 33.1% of those publications had at least one author citing their primary affiliation as NCAR.

Additional information was requested by NCAR leadership as part of the SVT report, including a list of the top 25 journals sorted by the publication frequency, the most cited publications, the most frequent collaborating institutions by frequency of unique co-author institution, and the top subject areas extracted from subject keywords in the publication metadata. These additional metrics stimulated a variety of lively discussions about the scholarly impact and reach of NCAR science. Because the Library was not directly involved in producing the *comprehensive* SVT reports that were distributed to each NSF team – which included far more than metrics – all of the metrics-specific data were organized into spreadsheets for easy browsing and quick access to relevant facts that were incorporated into the formatted and distributed comprehensive reports.

SVT Metrics Outcomes. The scope, scale, and timeline of the SVT metrics provided the first major test of the metrics capabilities the Library's first major test of the metrics capabilities it had been developing in the months leading up to the SVT reports. While the *outcomes* of the metrics themselves were of great importance to NCAR leadership and to the NSF SVT reports, for the Library the *process* of developing and producing the metrics was of greatest importance. There were three areas that were especially important to strengthening the process that was to be formalized later as part of the library's metrics offering. First, the role of collaboration became a central area of focus. Before the SVT metrics, the traditional publication curation model of the Library assumed that the production of publication sets was largely the role of the Library, and perhaps with meaningful contribution from domain experts. In the case of the SVT metrics, not only was the scale of the publication lists beyond the capabilities of the NCAR Library staff, the timeline did not allow for any staff to orient themselves to the individual requirements of each thematic area to contribute meaningfully. This was a necessary but important shift, and it turned the requirements of building relevant publication sets onto the domain experts. Because there were several experts assigned to each thematic area, this still yielded high-quality and relevant outcomes. This shift also placed focus on each team's collaborative relationship with the Library, increasing the communication about the collection process as each expert team independently developed their publication sets (Picture 1).

The data volume of the SVT metrics required the Library to automate the tools to access the underlying metadata from the various data providers. This automation fell into three distinct areas: (1) *pre-processing* the list of DOIs by de-duplicating and verifying correct DOI format, (2) *extracting* metadata for each publication for storage in a database, and (3) *analyzing* the metadata for individual and aggregate metrics. All primary metadata were sourced from Crossref and Web of Science, which were both accessed programmatically through their respective APIs. Since there were so many publications, automated processes often ran for many hours, and on several occasions service limits were

Scholarly Metrics at NCAR   25

Modeling and Data Assimilation Publications Fact Sheet
2005-2015 User Publication Analysis

About the Publications:
• Publications were found by searching NCAR's OpenSky Institutional Repository. This collection represents NCAR's refereed publications from 2005 to 2015;
• Also collected from Thomson Reuters Web of Science Index;
• Models captured by the publication list include, but not limited to, CAM-chem, MOZART, WACCM, WRF-chem, CESM and WRF;
• Others were derived from internally maintained research bibliographies.

5023 Total Peer-Reviewed Publications
8,904 Unique Authors
6.2 Avg. Authors/Pub
2,110 Unique Institutions
20.9 Avg. Citations/Pub
105,076 Total Citations
13.6 Avg. Citation/Pub in Atmospheric Sciences

Top 100 Institutions with the Greatest Number of Authors Citing NCAR resources*

Top 10 Impact Factor Journals by Pub Count
J. Clim.; IF 4.4, 389 pubs
Atmos.Chem. Phys.; IF 5.1, 347 pubs
Geophys. Res. Lett.; IF 4.2, 316 pubs
Clim. Dyn.; IF 4.7, 159 pubs
ApJ; IF 6.0, 119 pubs
Geosci. Model Dev.; IF 3.7, 72 pubs
J. Hydrometeorol.; IF 3.6, 59 pubs
Environ. Res. Lett.; IF 3.9, 47 pubs
J. Adv. Model Earth Sy.; IF 4.9, 45 pubs
Biogeosciences; IF 4.0, 40 pubs

Top 10 Institutions by Author Count
1. University of Colorado — 848
2. NOAA — 748
3. Pacific NW Natl Lab — 699
4. Chinese Acad Sci — 616
5. NASA — 560
6. Univ Wisconsin — 328
7. Univ Washington — 288
8. Univ Calif Berkeley — 236
9. Lawrence Livermore Natl Lab — 235
10. Caltech — 230

Most Common Topics

* One pin per citation, does not include duplicates

Compiled Spring 2016

Picture 1: An NCAR fact sheet developed for a slide presentation at an NSF SVT review of the NCAR modeling publications and scholarship. This example shows the use of library-generated metrics customized by others to specialized outputs

reached for the external APIs (e.g., requests per hour and account rate limits). No automation or programmatic tools were built to push the completed and analyzed metrics data of step 3 back into the Google Sheets, but it was considered as a future enhancement to support workflows that relied on Google Sheets.

Automation was necessary to commence the data collection and metrics analysis, but human intervention was critical to *complete* the analysis for several reasons. First, prior to the SVT requests, the metrics capabilities of the Library had only been tested with the supercomputer analysis, and hence data collection was confined to the initial API which had been developed. Much of the additional automation software required to complete the SVT metrics analysis was still under active development, being prototyped, or needing testing, and some of the software was error-prone, inefficient or required additional validation to confirm accuracy and reliability. Second, the specific needs of the SVT metrics required some metrics be obtained elsewhere or directly curated by human experts. For example, the expected cites per publication was a metric that was obtained elsewhere (Web of Science) and yet it was necessary to contextualize the outcomes of the SVT metrics. Finally, humans serve a necessary role in curation of publication lists. While there are many ongoing efforts to automate publication classification through text analytics and machine learning (many of them very successful), there are nuances in publications which are not easily recognized by machines. For example, machines still struggle to robustly detect publications in specialized domains where computational models (such as weather or climate models) are central to the results of the publication. Though citation of a computational model (or the reference publication(s) for a model) may serve as a weak indicator that a publication *used* the model, other features which may help distinguish publications vary so much that unreliable results render machine classification inadequate when compared to human experts. As these automated approaches improve, the decision to choose human curation over machine automation might be determined by the scale of the task to the tolerance for inaccuracies. In the case of the SVT analysis, accuracy was critically important and including inappropriate publications outside the specialized domains represented by NCAR would not have been acceptable.

Lessons Learned. Although the Library considered the final outcome of the SVT metrics a success, *process refinement* and *benchmarking* gained renewed attention after the work was completed. In the area of process refinement, the Library recognized the need to remain flexible and adaptable when engaging scholarly metrics requests. Specifically, the Library recognized that in many cases domain experts, especially in highly specialized scientific domains such as climate science, are eager and willing to curate their own publications. When the metrics are designed to answer explicit questions about the publications, process flexibility permits domain experts to focus on high-quality, targeted curation and the Library to concentrate on quickly delivering automated metrics. When metrics are designed to be more exploratory and when there are fewer concrete objectives, the Library can often provide guidance during the curation process or become directly involved in it. The Library also recognized that improving repeatability was the easiest path to process improvement, and that deliberate and consistent efforts were necessary to formalize the entire metrics process so that it could be communicated, monitored, and evaluated. The formalized metrics workflow including the constituent process activities and stakeholders is discussed in detail later in the chapter.

As the SVT metrics began to circulate among both broader NCAR and NSF audiences, a growing number of questions emerged about the *meaning* of the metrics. For example, it was unclear to many what to *expect* from the average number of collaborators per paper. There were repeated concerns about the average citations per publication – a concern that has been a persistent focus in traditional bibliometrics – and about the weight each metric should carry. Furthermore, the duration of the analysis, when contextualized against the changes which had occurred not only within NCAR, but also within each scientific field of study, raised even more questions about how to appropriately interpret the results and how to improve them in the future by placing them within a germane context. This latter point was also acknowledged by domain expert curators and underscored the indispensibility of human domain experts. To address these questions the Library performed an analysis of NAR publications over the same timespan as the SVT publications – recall, the NAR publications are NCAR-authored publications curated and compiled annually by the Library – and used the results as a benchmark for comparison. The NAR benchmark proved to be useful, but was very different in many ways from the thematic SVT publication sets since the NCAR authorship requirement of NAR publications considerably restricted the size and co-author composition. Nonetheless, the NAR benchmark demonstrated an acknowledgment that it was important to address the questions about the context of all the SVT metrics.

These lessons set the stage for the final NCAR Library metrics case study in the next section.

EarthCube Community Metrics

The NSF has broadly supported initiatives to develop cyberinfrastructure that support scientific research. The EarthCube (EC) Initiative is one such project which received initial funding in 2011 to "transform geoscience research by developing cyberinfrastructure to improve access, sharing, visualization, and analysis of all forms of geosciences data and related resources." It was specifically tasked with developing a community-governed approach to face the increasingly complex landscape of problems in "Earth, hydrosphere, atmosphere and space environment systems." The project is centered on computational models, software, tools, and infrastructure technologies which foster standards-based technologies that focus on interoperability, improving data integration, visualization and analysis, in addition to improving and democratizing access to data. The community now consists of thousands of contributors to over 50 funded projects, including nearly 32 actively funded projects as of the beginning of 2019.

Though the EC Initiative was funded as a cyberinfrastructure project and produced many kinds of outputs, publications were an important vehicle for disseminating results and reporting project outcomes. The EarthCube Science Support Office (ESSO), which is managed and operated within UCAR, approached the NCAR Library with a request for metrics analysis of the publication rate of each funded project. Data for the request were contributed in part by ESSO project management and by self-reported publication sets from EC project principal investigators. The ESSO also had a detailed list of the NSF grant identifiers associated with each EC-funded project, and the NCAR Library suggested this list be used to verify and augment the lists that had already been developed. The NSF manages an online grants database which contains a list of *reported* peer-reviewed publications as required by annual status reporting. The Library was able to use these identifiers to add (and verify) publications on the lists already obtained by ESSO, discussed further in the next section. Since many of the outputs of the EC community did *not* include publications, the ESSO also gathered information about other project outcomes.

The metrics needs of the ESSO were not as clear as in the previous case studies already presented in this work. No specific questions had been set forth for analysis – the ESSO was primarily interested in only understanding what the peer-reviewed publication metrics were for funded projects – there were no other specific questions, targets, or assumptions given. This exploratory approach was also overshadowed by another fact about the EC funding program: $30.4M in funds had been allocated to the EC projects under analysis. This led to an interest in a *publications-per-dollar* metric, which can lead to over-simplistic and reductionist views, and detract attention from the more important *context* of the metrics. The Library repeatedly maintained the position that pursuing a single simplistic metric was not necessary, and that it was more important to look at every metric within its appropriate context – whatever the metrics outcomes were.

In all, the analysis involved data from 52 EC-funded projects since program inception in 2011. This data included some 90 unique peer-reviewed publications that yielded valid DOIs. Other project outputs totaled over 350 discrete output products, split between posters, conference and meeting talks, software, and publications for which no DOI existed (or no metadata existed for the DOIs given). It should be noted that as in prior analyses, the DOI for a publication was crucially important since all of the metrics automation was built upon programmatically extracting and computationally analyzing metadata from metadata service providers.

Because of the much smaller publication counts that could be used for metrics analysis – due in part to the size of the community, the duration of the funded programs and as discovered later, the *types* of outputs expected of projects based on their activities – the Library suggested that altmetrics be included in the publication metrics analysis. This suggestion was made in part because the Library was expanding its automation of altmetric score extraction, and as part of offering broader contexts of publication metrics designed to capture social media attention. While considered *emerging metrics*, these altmetrics do provide another lens that bring focus to the context of publications that may have less time to accumulate traditional citations or that may be of such timeliness that they garner significant social media attention. The Library felt that at least *considering* altmetrics was a valuable exercise and that they could be used *as necessary* to supplement the results of the traditional bibliometrics analysis. Finally, the Library cautioned that even altmetric attention may also need *contextualizing*. For example, some communities have more active online social media communities skewing altmetric "attention" toward some publications over.

A final note must be made of an especially unique aspect of the EC project output that hints at the expanded contexts scholarly metrics must consider as new analysis techniques are developed. Several EC projects were focused primarily on developing community software and data products, which also contained DOIs now being recognized as an essential identifier to promote findability and citation of software and data. EC projects which had minted DOIs for software and data were included for analysis, and while these did not (at the time of the analysis) materially contribute to the metrics outcomes, they reinforced an important signal that these traceable project outputs will become increasingly important to future metrics.

Metrics Outcomes Summary. The EC metrics for peer-reviewed publications spanned five years (2012 to 2017, and of the 95 DOIs found for the publications produced by the EC community, Web of Science metadata matched only

41 of those DOIs. These 41 publications gathered 75 total citations, amounting to 1.83 citations per publication. As anticipated, the small number of *peer-reviewed* publications under-represented the activities of the EC projects, but more interestingly, the publication venues covered by Web of Science significantly reduced the citation-eligible publications to fewer than 45% of the DOIs under exploration. This unexpected outcome was the result of the publication venues typical of the EC community not being indexed by Web of Science. The emerging metrics produced by Altmetric.com mentions covered 26 DOIs, of which nearly 10 (38%) had attention scores greater than the 75th percentile of Altmetric scores. This was a surprising result, since only one publication in the analyzed set produced more than 10 citations. Even more surprising was that three of those 10 publications were within the top one-percentile of Altmetric Attention Scores and were published in 2017 (the year of the analysis).

There were only a few software projects and datasets which had DOIs, and none of them had accumulated citations at the time of the analysis, but this finding required an important qualification. For some time, software and data projects have been broadly encouraged to mint DOIs so they may reap the benefits of formal citation; however, the *uptake* of formally citing such DOIs has been slow, and only recently received widespread attention for further study. Authors are frequently reminded to cite these resources appropriately, and though the growth of this behavior is just now being seen, there are indications that many authors are aware of the importance of acknowledging these often ignored, but *fundamental* resources. Though there was no evidence the EC projects were formally cited with these identifiers, as tools for recognizing and tracking these identifiers improve, it is expected that in the near future, citation counts for popular software and datasets may eclipse even the most widely cited publications.

There was a lingering concern, however, that the ratio of peer-reviewed publications to *other* project outputs would underwhelm the metrics in a way that would diminish their impact. The final metrics included the broad spectrum of outputs from the EC community, which included the nearly 350 posters, talks, and other important artifacts of value to the community. The reality that was being uncovered was that the EC projects were not driven by peer-reviewed publications as much as by the needs of each community relying on the infrastructure tools being designed. Indeed, since EC projects were designed to *support* research, project priorities were often driven by the needs of a particular research community rather than on research about the tools being developed. Furthermore, as a project early in its development, and having only been funded in earnest for six years prior to the initial metrics evaluation, it was not realistic to expect neither a large number of publications nor citations would have resulted.

More interestingly, hints emerged of a phenomenon similar to that found in the supercomputer metrics analysis. Because most EC projects functioned in service to broader communities, the *traceable impact* was much more complex and nuanced. Projects like these rely on researchers and authors that make use of their project outcomes (e.g., tools, models, and software) to acknowledge, cite, and give credit to those outcomes. Undocumented and uncited, these important project outcomes are weakened and much like what was uncovered in the analysis done over the EC publications, the contexts within which these projects live and thrive become unclear. Funders and decision-makers who do not understand or are unaware of those contexts, risk being misled into poor conclusions when they fall back to metrics which are widely known or familiar – citation counts, publication counts, or even publications-per-dollar.

Lessons Learned. The EC metrics analysis gave the Library a unique opportunity to help develop an appropriate metrics profile that accurately reflected the context of a project for which there was low support for a publication-heavy metrics analysis. The metrics analysis request could have ended in the early data collection phase when the publication count fell below 100 – expectations for such a small number of publications would already be low. The role of the Library, however, was (and is) to collect the data and evaluate the metrics where they stand. In addition to that, the Library must comprehensively, accurately, and objectively seek to develop the appropriate contexts around the data and metrics under analysis. This lesson cannot be overstated, since it is far easier to halt further analysis when traditional notions of metrics fail to uncover impressive results.

The application of altmetrics on such a small set of publications expanded the analysis in meaningful ways, and though altmetrics must be couched carefully and balanced with other metrics, they offer valuable insights that would otherwise go ignored or be dismissed in light of more familiar traditional metrics. The surprising outcomes of the EC altmetrics emphasize their importance, especially when they are appropriately contextualized. Without them, the Library would not have been able to demonstrate that several publications which had not accumulated many traditional citations had impressively high Altmetric.com rankings. Furthermore, publications that were not yet indexed by the tools the Library was using (Web of Science) showed Altmetric Attention Scores that demonstrated attention that would otherwise have gone unnoticed. The publishing cycles and tools that analyze citation counts require more time to detect the attention signals that altmetrics uncovered shortly after publications appear online. These important signals cannot be ignored, and as these metrics mature they will play an increasingly substantial role in scholarly metrics despite the criticisms lodged against them. Just like traditional bibliometrics before, altmetrics will be adapted to take their place within the spectrum of scholarly metrics tools and techniques.

The publications that were assembled for the EC metrics were largely self-reported and managed voluntarily. This is the prevailing paradigm for publication management at NCAR, and presumably similar laboratories and research organizations with comparable complexity. This method of collecting publications is often augmented by libraries and information science experts within the Library, especially those skilled at tools for ongoing publication management. These human efforts to manage publications are being scaled by machines, and in the case of the EC project, augmented by machine-accessible datasets that expose publications to supplement, enhance, or validate human-curated and managed publication sets. In the case of this project, the NSF-managed awards database proved to be an essential tool to both validate and supplement self-reported publications. The Library took accessing this database one step forward by building an automated tool to programmatically access the API exposing this data. This facilitated an automated mechanism to validate self-reported publications, but it also served to expand the publication set by exposing unreported publications. Finally, this automation allowed for the project grant identifiers and corresponding publications to be linked into a single report that uncovered a granular view of the project-specific publication metrics, which were linked with other project outcomes and assets into a more complete view of all funded projects.

The initial data collection occurred in 2017, and in early 2018 new data were added reflecting the results of renewed, program-level calls to update publications and project outcomes. The updated publication set uncovered gaps in the original data, where, for example, projects had incomplete or inaccurate publication sets. Overall, with the new data the total publications ballooned from 95 to 145 (an increase of 52%), and the number of publications with Web of Science metadata increased 88% from 41 to 78. Of note within the updated set, was the marked increase in citation accumulation among the most highly cited publications and among all publications. For example, in the original metrics analysis, the most highly cited publication had accumulated only 13 citations. Less than a year later, the same publication (which remained the most cited publication on the updated list) had double the number of citations at 26. The citations-per-publication increased nearly fourfold from 1.8 to 6.8. Furthermore, the most frequently cited publications had shifted, the reason for which was not well understood, though it was conjectured that the shift could be attributed to more robust publication reporting, extended index coverage by Web of Science, improved NSF database coverage of reported publications, among other factors. These changes draw attention to the uncertainty of citation counts, the time required for them to accumulate, and the value of altmetrics as tools to add breadth, depth, and context publication metrics.

For the Library, the EC metrics showed the importance of analyzing metrics on their own and exploring available data over the widest range of analyses to build a rich context for whatever metrics *do* materialize. The inclusion of altmetrics and the expansion of the original EC publication set strengthened the overall metrics profile for the project, which helped to demonstrate the importance of the traditional metrics, altmetrics, and other project outcomes which could not be captured by either. The initial concerns that the available "traditional" metrics would fail to show the importance of the work being done within each EC group were reconciled by balancing those metrics with altmetrics and metrics related to conference talks and posters. Further, demonstrating the impact of all project outcomes required that the full context of the outcomes (e.g. other project assets and software) be illuminated, including re-casting each project against the program purpose and community activities.

The NCAR Library Scholarly Metrics Workflow

The case studies described in the prior section led the NCAR Library to develop and formalize a metrics workflow process to reflect the lessons learned and accommodate future needs as necessary. The workflow captures the essential components of the research metrics process without imposing *specific* tools or technologies so that it could be implemented within whatever environment or operating framework required. As learned from the case studies previously discussed, such flexibility is necessary since none of the cases was exactly the same, nor had the same needs or desired outcomes.

The workflow process is distributed across four major activities: *planning*, *managing*, *analyzing*, and *reporting*. Transitions into and out of each activity are loosely triggered by the completion of the subordinate activities within each major activity, but as can be seen in Fig. 1, these activities do not necessarily need to be completely in sequence, and the overall workflow process is circular and itself does not require one activity to be fully completed before the next activity begins. Activities might be done in parallel when there are partially completed activities. For example, a *complete* publication set is not necessary to perform an analysis, and depending on the technology and tools used to perform analyses, updates between publication sets and metrics could be continuous and instantaneous.

The workflow process requires a number of human interventions and stakeholders to be engaged in each major activity. For example, during planning, several key stakeholders are required, such as lab managers and leadership invested in the metrics. Stakeholders will vary based on activity; for example, the collection of publications sets could be performed by library and information science experts, but the activity could also be performed by administrative personnel or

Fig. 1: The NCAR metrics workflow from initial planning to the automation of metrics to reporting

domain experts, as occurred with the NSF SVT metrics. The workflow is flexible enough to adapt to whatever configuration of personnel is available and appropriate.

The circular flow of activities accentuates the importance of ongoing reflection and adjustment throughout each activity. Linearity often undermines the fluidity required to adapt and respond to the ambiguities that are inherent in metrics analysis. Thus, it is implied that returning to an activity after it has been completed is anticipated as much as it is expected.

Planning

In response to the metrics experiences previously described, though the planning activity should be as formal as necessary, it requires flexibility and whenever possible metrics prioritization. In each case presented in this chapter, different planning scenarios were necessary and the planning activity requires careful attention and prioritization based on the timeline and expectations of the metrics stakeholders (e.g., those accessing the final data, developing or preparing reports and presentations, and presentations including metrics analyses). A review of all existing data sources, while not necessary, should receive some attention if time permits. It is not unusual to uncover data that is already curated by a yet unidentified or unnamed group or individual. For example, *someone* (i.e., individual researcher, administrator, etc.) in nearly every research organization has a specialized research publication list that might shorten the time to compile a comprehensive publication list, and in many cases, these specialized lists focus on hard-to-qualify subdomains of interest. Though formally drafting and writing a plan is not required, doing so raises the level of commitment, expectation, and understanding of the metrics process. During the planning activity, it is important to engage all of the necessary stakeholders, managers, and leadership and fully integrate them into the process. If necessary, the plan should involve a commitment to specific deliverables, whether they be formal reports, spreadsheets, raw data files, access to data via APIs, and so on. For metrics that are ongoing, any formalized plans should be reviewed and regularly updated as deliverables are changed, completed, or reprioritized.

Managing

Managing large publication sets is competently handled by numerous bibliographic management software tools, yet depending on the complexity and specific requirements, this management may require other tools. For example, while many metadata providers include grant data (where it exists) within the metadata for a publication, such data are not guaranteed to exist. Furthermore, many institutions track information with internal identifiers so they can be integrated easily with data already in enterprise resource management systems (e.g., human resource tracking, financial planning, and management systems). To accommodate the organization and linking of publications to other systems, a flexible system should be developed. The NCAR Library developed a programmatic service

API which generalized both the data collection and the metrics so that data could be stored and retrieved for internal library needs and external enterprise-level needs (though there has yet been little opportunity to integrate the API into broader NCAR-wide systems). The capability is nonetheless an important function of a comprehensive metrics system which may require such broad enterprise integration.

Curating publication sets has been a traditional role filled by research library and information science experts, yet in each of the three cases mentioned in this chapter, all of the curation began as an activity *outside* the Library. This paradigm allowed the Library to scale its metrics offerings in a way that would not have been possible if the curation activity was the sole responsibility of the Library. By leveraging subject matter expertise of external partners and broadly available tools for bibliographic management, the Library was able to develop advanced analysis technologies and focus on value-added *services*.

Analyzing

Performing analysis of publication sets can be an ongoing activity and the capabilities of the analysis depend largely on the technologies available. Again, the workflow shown in Fig. 1 does not prescribe a specific technology or tool, and could be built atop custom tools, or off-the-shelf tools. For example, Clarivate provides analytics through the *InCites* product, which permits the end user to build and customize basic dashboards for exploration of large publications sets. The impermanence of these dashboards and their configuration options may restrict many users with advanced needs or those requiring complex queries against the underlying data. Furthermore, these vendor tools limit integrating and synthesizing publication metrics with other data sources (internal or external enterprise data). The NCAR Library anticipated these problems by developing an API which abstracted the data and its access. To facilitate library-internal and external requests for data, the API generates data payloads that can be reshaped by the requester and simplifies quick access to summary information about publication sets. It also provides convenient programmatic access to aggregate publication set metrics such as author, institution, subject, and keyword frequencies. Though the API has not yet been fully exercised outside the Library, the long-term plan is to make it open and available as a service for NCAR-internal access so that the data can be integrated as necessary with other NCAR enterprise systems.

Reporting

Reporting is a necessary activity in any metrics workflow, but so much variance exists in reporting output formats, update frequency, access controls and a myriad of other customizations, that reporting can often be a time-consuming and resource-intensive activity on its own. The NCAR Library provided basic graphical views of the data in each of the case studies here, but did not expend resources to develop additional functionality or tools to support customizable reports. The stakeholders in each case, either had their own reporting strategy and output format in mind, or had little need for more than was offered by the Library. The ideal reporting activity, however, should engage the stakeholders of the reports and identify where the appropriate reporting opportunities are. Many dynamic systems consume data from other services (via APIs) and provide their end users with whatever customizations they require. Within the framework of a model like this, it may be less resource intensive to focus just on functionality and metadata technologies that deliver relevant reporting data to another service through an API.

The metrics workflow here does not capture every activity involved in developing metrics; rather, it builds a flexible and activity-driven framework for capturing the most important activities and stakeholders in scholarly metrics. It can be adapted to a variety of other data and inputs that may be available to the Library and will be refashioned as more experiences are gained from interacting with future metrics requests.

Lessons Learned on the Future of Scholarly Metrics

Scholarly metrics are a necessary and important tool for research organizations and are increasingly important in strategic planning, resource planning, and decision-making for collaboration and funding opportunities. Libraries have always played a vital role in the collection, dissemination, and interpretation of scholarly metrics, but their role is shifting toward developing technologies and technical *services* around those metrics. Instead of spending the bulk of their efforts on *curation*, libraries are expanding their energy toward *technical integrations* that facilitate metrics data collection, management, analysis, and reporting.

The NCAR Library began building metrics services initially to support groups at all levels of the organization, not knowing fully what kinds of metrics requests to anticipate. As detailed in this chapter, these metrics case studies varied greatly from small exploratory metrics to large-scale metrics involving a variety of inputs and stakeholders. The role of the Library was a technical one – scoped to focus on the necessary technical tools to process data for metrics analysis. The Library realized that the bulk of its resources needed to be directed toward the software tools and integrations to make metrics data available, rather than on its traditional role in curation of data inputs. Recognizing this directly influenced the development of the NCAR Library Metrics Workflow introduced earlier in the chapter and since then the workflow has become the standard way the Library plans for and engages new requests for metrics.

Developing scholarly metrics capabilities should be a key service of any research library today. This chapter presented several distinct cases that represented different needs and contexts for scholarly metrics. A technology-agnostic framework for structuring the activities from planning to reporting was also presented. In exploring the various cases for metrics, a few indicators emerge that hint at where metrics to *quantify* and *qualify* the value, importance, and impact of scholarly activities may evolve. First, tracing the instruments and infrastructure supporting scholarly research, such as supercomputer facilities or instruments such as satellites, will become more prominent. In the era of cloud computing, a real risk exists that in order to stay competitive, computing infrastructures, especially, will become hyper-specialized (and hence more valuable) to deeply serve their communities. Similarly, as Internet of Things and ubiquitous and inexpensive sensors become unimaginably valuable research tools, new opportunities will materialize to develop metrics for how these new tools map onto the outcomes of modern scholarship. As with software, tracing and developing metrics will be a challenge that cannot be ignored – as these tools and technologies will profoundly influence, support, and shape future scholarship. Tracing resources will also become easier since minting and citing persistent identifiers for every kind of resource will become commonplace.

Though much of this chapter embraces the *technological enablers* of scholarly metrics and the future that lies ahead, it is unlikely that libraries will acquiesce the most important role as the unprejudiced arbiter of scholarly metrics – a role they have played since the beginning and one they will continue to play in the metrics landscape of tomorrow. The volume and complexity of the inputs to modern scholarly metrics may increase, but the necessary contextualization of those metrics will require human interpreters. Perhaps even more so than today, human decision-making will enrich and enable the future of scholarly metrics and deepen the essential role of context.

References

Borgman, C. L., & Furner, J. (2002). Scholarly communication and bibliometrics. *Annual Review of Information Science and Technology*, *36*(1), 2–72. DOI:10.1002/aris.1440360102

Costas, R., Zahedi, Z., & Wouters, P. (2015). Do "altmetrics" correlate with citations? Extensive comparison of altmetric indicators with citations from a multidisciplinary perspective. *Journal of the Association for Information Science and Technology*, *66*(10), 2003–2019. DOI:10.1002/asi.23309

Garfield, E. (1979). *Citation indexing: Its theory and application in science, technology, and humanities*. Philadelphia, PA: ISI Press.

Gutzman, K. E., Bales, M. E., Belter, C. W., Chambers, T., Chan, L., Holmes, K. L., ... Wheeler, T. R. (2018). Research evaluation support services in biomedical libraries. *Journal of the Medical Library Association*, *106*(1), 1–14. DOI:10.5195/JMLA.2018.205

Hart, D., Rishel, M., & Nychka, D. (2016). Estimating the accuracy of user surveys for assessing the impact of HPC systems. In K. Gaither (Ed.), *Proceedings of the XSEDE16 conference on diversity, big data, and science at scale* (pp. 18:1–18:7). New York, NY: ACM. DOI:10.1145/2949550.2949583

Haustein, S. (2016). Grand challenges in altmetrics: Heterogeneity, data quality and dependencies. *Scientometrics*, *108*(1), 413–423. DOI:10.1007/s11192-016-1910-9

Ilik, V., Conlon, M., Triggs, G., White, M., Javed, M., Brush, M., ... Holmes, K. L. (2018). OpenVIVO: Transparency in scholarship. *Frontiers in Research Metrics and Analytics*, *2*, 12. DOI:10.3389/frma.2017.00012

Mayernik, M. S., Hart, D. L., Maull, K. E., & Weber, N. M. (2017). Assessing and tracing the outcomes and impact of research infrastructures. *Journal of the Association for Information Science and Technology*, *68*(6), 1341–1359. DOI:10.1002/asi.23721

Milojević, S., & Leydesdorff, L. (2013). Information metrics (iMetrics): A research specialty with a socio-cognitive identity? *Scientometrics*, *95*(1), 141–157. DOI:10.1007/s11192-012-0861-z

Moed, H. F. (2005). *Citation analysis in research evaluation*. Dordrecht, The Netherlands: Springer.

Nicolaisen, J. (2007). Citation analysis. *Annual Review of Information Science and Technology*, *41*(1), 609–641. DOI:10.1002/aris.2007.1440410120

Piwowar, H. (2013). Altmetrics: Value all research products. *Nature*, *493*, 159. DOI:10.1038/493159a

Tague, J. (1988). What's the use of bibliometrics? In L. Egghe & R. Rousseau (Eds.), *Informetrics 87/88* (pp. 271–278). New York, NY: Elsevier.

Tahamtan, I., & Bornmann, L. (2018). Core elements in the process of citing publications: Conceptual overview of the literature. *Journal of Informetrics*, *12*(1), 203–216. DOI:10.1016/j.joi.2018.01.002

Appendix

THE STORY OF CISL SUPERCOMPUTER PUBLICATIONS
2008-2013 USER SURVEY PUBLICATION ANALYSIS

THE DATA

- Peer-reviewed publications generated from the use of NCAR Super-computer Resources.
- Gathered from user reported survey data (~25% mean response rate) of peer-reviewed publications.
- Includes publications of Yellowstone and Bluefire supercomputer users.
- Respondents represent a population sample of nearly 75% of accounts using >50 core hours in survey year.
- Metrics may be combined with supercomputer utilization for further analysis.

THE ANALYSIS

803 TOTAL PEER-REVIEWED PUBLICATIONS*

547 TOTAL UNIQUE INSTITUTIONS

13007 TOTAL CITATIONS

16.20 CITATIONS PER PUBLICATION

1202 TIMES THE TOP 5 NON-NCAR LED PAPERS WERE CITED

420 citations (Univ Maryland lead): Carton, J. A., & Giese, B. S. (2008). A Reanalysis of Ocean Climate Using Simple Ocean Data Assimilation (SODA). Monthly Weather Review, 136(8), 2999–3017. doi:10.1175/2007mwr1978.1

246 citations (Georgia Inst Technol lead): Di Lorenzo, E., Schneider, N., Cobb, K. M., Franks, P. J. S., Chhak, K., Miller, A. J., ... Rivière, P. (2008). North Pacific Gyre Oscillation links ocean climate and ecosystem change. Geophys. Res. Lett., 35(8). doi:10.1029/2007gl032838

238 citations (Rutgers Univ lead): Haidvogel, D. B., Arango, H., Budgell, W. P., Cornuelle, B. D., Curchitser, E., Di Lorenzo, E., ... Wilkin, J. (2008). Ocean forecasting in terrain-following coordinates: Formulation and skill assessment of the Regional Ocean Modeling System. Journal of Computational Physics, 227(7), 3595–3624. doi:10.1016/j.jcp.2007.06.016

160 citations (Chinese Acad Sci/Univ Wisconsin lead): Liu, Z., Otto-Bliesner, B. L., He, F., Brady, E. C., Tomas, R., Clark, P. U., ... Cheng, J. (2009). Transient Simulation of Last Deglaciation with a New Mechanism for Bolling-Allerod Warming. Science, 325(5938), 310–314. doi:10.1126/science.1171041

138 citations (Univ Calif Irvine lead): Randerson, J. T., Hoffman, F. M., Thornton, P. E., Mahowald, N. M., Lindsay, K., Lee, Y.-H., ... Fung, I. Y. (2009). Systematic assessment of terrestrial biogeochemistry in coupled climate-carbon models. Global Change Biology, 15(10), 2462–2484. doi:10.1111/j.1365-2486.2009.01912.x

MOST PROLIFIC LEAD INSTITUTIONS

Institution	Total Lead Pubs	Cites Per Lead Pub
Univ Colorado	44	13.39
Univ Wisconsin	34	19.12
Ctr Ocean Land Atmosphere Studies	22	12.55
Univ Michigan	22	16.55
Univ Washington	22	18.82
Colorado State Univ	21	12.81
Florida State Univ	18	5.61
Cornell Univ	16	19.31
Univ Calif Berkeley	16	22.00
Columbia Univ	14	14.57
Univ Calif Los Angeles	14	10.21
George Mason Univ	13	6.38
Univ Delaware	13	13.15
Univ Maryland	13	50.54
Univ Calif Irvine	11	32.73
NOAA	10	22.70

TOTAL CITATIONS PER YEAR

2007	2008	2009	2010	2011	2012	2013
413	2575	2298	2761	1739	1946	1275

MOST CITED LEAD INSTITUTIONS
*: Int'l Affiliate, †: UCAR Member

Institution	Lead Pubs	Cites Per Lead Pub	Total Pubs
Georgia Inst Technol†	3	89.67	10
Univ Sheffield	1	79.00	2
Argonne Natl Lab	1	67.00	4
WHOI†	1	67.00	1
Univ Toronto*	1	66.00	4
Seoul Natl Univ*	2	53.00	7
NASA GSFC	1	53.00	1
Royal Netherlands Meteorol Inst KNMI			
De Bilt	1	52.00	1
Univ Maryland†	13	50.54	28
Dalian Univ Technol	1	49.00	1
Rutgers State Univ†	6	47.83	26
Univ Lancaster	1	46.00	1
Desert Res Inst†	1	44.00	4

PUBLICATIONS PER YEAR

2007	2008	2009	2010	2011	2012	2013
19	69	92	125	132	177	189

2095 TOTAL UNIQUE AUTHORS

5.13 AUTHORS PER PUBLICATION

PROLIFIC AUTHORS (by pub count)
†: ASP Fellow, ‡: NCAR Faculty Fellowship, 2005

18	L. Wang	Univ Delaware
17	N. Mahowald	Cornell Univ
14	B. Kirtman	Univ Miami
13	E. Maloney‡	Colorado State Univ
13	S. Vavrus‡	Univ Wisconsin

TOP LEAD AUTHORS (by pub count)

8	S. Vavrus	Univ Wisconsin
6	T. Krishnamurti	Florida State Univ
5	Z. Liu†	Univ Wisconsin
5	Z. Wang	Univ Illinois
4	G. Jin	Chinese Acad Sci
4	B. Kirtman	Univ Miami

116 TOTAL UNIQUE JOURNALS

Journal	Total Pubs
Journal of Climate	122
J. Geophys. Res.	100
Geophysical Research Letters	67
Mon. Wea. Rev.	55
Atmos. Chem. Phys.	51
Journal of the Atmospheric Sciences	42

31 DISTINCT PUBLISHERS

Publisher	Total Pubs
American Meteorological Society	281
Wiley-Blackwell	232
Copernicus GmbH	69
Springer Science + Business Media	69
Elsevier BV	62
IOP Publishing	25

44 SUBJECT AREAS

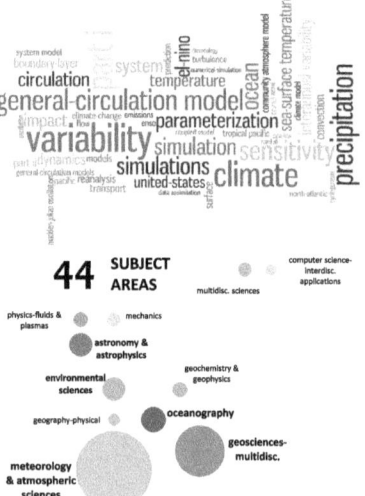

Chapter 3

New Metrics for Measuring Academic Research Outside the Ivory Tower

Kendra K. Levine

The need to demonstrate the value of research programs is critical for funding sustainability, particularly in the 21st century when research funding is rarely guaranteed beyond the life of a single project. Since the great economic crash of 2008, many research programs have also diversified their funding portfolios, which means cultivating new relationships with funders and potentially different objectives of research projects. Measuring the impact of academic research outside academia is critical to providing a holistic view of a research program, but the methods to do so are still being figured out and are largely context specific. Within the field of transportation, no metrics for measuring the impact of research have really been established. Readily available and easily measured metrics, like citations or other scholarly impact factors, are not entirely appropriate to assess these kinds of research, since they hew to a narrow academic setting. This chapter proposes a methodology to track and measure the impact of research conducted by the University of California Institute of Transportation Studies (UC-ITS), a multi-campus research organization at US Berkeley, UC Davis, UC Irvine, and UC Los Angeles (UCLA). This methodology can be used beyond academic settings across an number of disciplines related to transportation topics.

Research Impacts

Established Scholarly Metrics

Traditional scholarly metrics, for all their ills, have been established to describe the impact of academic research within academic venues. These methods can be considered acceptable for academic evaluation, like promotion and tenure cases, academic research program reviews, or grant applications. Scholarly metrics like journal impact factors (JIFs) are insufficient for demonstrating the impact of research beyond academia, especially since the mechanism to accept and publish research papers in academic journals (peer review) can be seen "as much of a lottery as a rational process" (Seglen, 1997, 314). Throughout the

1990s several researchers explored how journal and article citations could be used to evaluate research, though the tools available at the time were limited due to the maturity and sophistication of citation databases at that point (Taubes, 1993). In the intervening years a lot of progress has been made in developing systems and platforms to track citation data, but there is still a need for an open ecosystem for these data for more robust analysis outside vendor platforms or questionable black boxes like Google Scholar (Shotton, 2013). The JIF is still frequently cited and relied upon, despite established limitations in measuring anything about research beyond a raw number of citations (Seglen, 1997). There is merit to discussions about the possibilities of abandoning JIFs for evaluation purposes and developing a new, more deliberate and thoughtful approach for scholarly metrics, but JIFs are so entrenched that there is little chance of that happening at scale (Archambault & Larivière, 2009). The PLoS Medicine Editors (2016) published an editorial in 2006 about the potential gamification of impact factors, concluding that as scientific publishing is democratized and authors and readers have more options to engage outside the established (and tracked) publishing platforms, JIF will be less relevant:

> If authors are going to quote the impact factor of a journal, they should understand what it can and cannot measure. The opening up of the literature means that better ways of assessing papers and journals are coming – and we should embrace them (e291).

Any continued reliance on these metrics needs to account for their clear limitations and known problems. JIFs need to be contextualized as a reminder of what they actually measure, what they can represent, but more importantly what they cannot.

Using the same methodology for evaluating research impacts across disciplines is problematic because coverage in journal citation reports in Clarivate (formerly known as Institute for Scientiific Information [ISI]) Web of Science, and other citation tracking databases is not uniform across fields. In mathematics, for example, many of the leading journals are not indexed in Web of Science (Korevaar, 1996). Normalizing citation data for bibliometric research is one way to address subject-based limitations for comparisons, though that is not frequently done when research groups or departments are evaluating themselves or their peers (Bornmann, 2013). Proposed new metrics based on these normalization techniques, such as Source Normalized Impact Per Paper or Field-Weighted Citation Impact, could be widely adopted to provide a more fair evaluation tool across science (Kochetkov, 2018). However, any new measures should only be used if they actually add value to the evaluation process and are not simply another number to be gamed (Watermeyer & Hedgecoe, 2016). Despite (or because of) the proliferation of academic journals in transportation, the impact metrics for transportation literature range from barely measurable to decently respectable, though are still relatively small compared to other fields like medicine (Banister, 2014). Comparing JIFs across disciplines lacks nuance and assumes that all fields of research should be held to the same arbitrary standard, which is in essence a fool's game.

For many fields the demonstrable impact of research as applied outside university settings is far greater than could be measured by JIFs, *h*-indexes, or other scholarly metrics. Research output in the form of policies, new operations, improved systems which have impacts on society, the environment, and economy, have impact and reach extend far beyond academia. Comparing academic researchers and programs whose research is close to application and deployment solely using traditional scholarly metrics, such as bibliometric indicators, ignores other possible metrics to evaluate the impact of research. One reason is frequently these research outputs are published as some form of gray literature, such as technical reports, white papers, or policy briefs. As a result, impact is more difficult to track and measure since such documents are usually excluded from most scholarly metrics systems, and many citing references might be in other forms of gray literature, standards, or other kinds of working documents for different organizations. Google Scholar has proved to be useful in measuring the impact of these kinds of research outputs, by casting a wider net of tracked citations than Scopus or Web of Science (Haddaway, Collins, Coughlin, & Kirk, 2015). Google Scholar citations have many limitations though, since their accuracy and consistency is far from guaranteed (Falagas, Pitsouni, Malietzis, & Pappas, 2007). Altmetrics are another tool to measure the potential reach of research outside academic settings, though there are still many issues to work out, such as differentiating between buzz of people talking about new findings and actual impact of how those findings are used in the field (Bornmann, 2014).

There is also the fundamental issue of defining "impact" in an academic research context (Terämä, Smallman, Lock, Johnson, & Austwick, 2016). Different research disciplines have their own measures of impact, making any comparisons across them potentially contentious. Academics also have their own ideas of impact that likely differ from research funders and other stakeholders. Faculty and graduate students on the academic job market need to publish their research in highly ranked academic journals that are valued by promotion and tenure committees. The journals are not necessarily read by or even accessible to practitioners in the field who are involved in setting the research agenda, developing and advising on policy, and deploying new processes or technology into the field. Different publication venues and formats will reach and appeal to different audiences, and therefore must be accounted for and tracked, to fully assess the impact of a research project or program. As noted before, Web of Science and other scholarly metrics tools do not work for gray literature because they are not part of those ecosystems. By its very nature, gray literature is accessible (and diffuse), because it is widely available to the public on the web. This is important because practitioners by-and-large work for public agencies or private companies, not universities or colleges with access to scholarly publications through libraries. Thus, accounting for citations in gray literature is necessary when looking at research impact beyond academia. For some fields, such as agriculture and aerospace, forms of gray literature are largely respected and expected to be used and cited in research (Auger, 1998). For public policy development and analysis, gray literature is a vital resource used in conjunction with scholarly sources (Lawrence, Houghton, Thomas, & Weldon, 2014). Currently, tracking citations in that fashion is a very labor-intensive task in the vein of finding needles in haystacks. This is why people rely on Google Scholar even though it is a deeply flawed tool with questionable reliability.

Societal Impacts

In 1945, Vannevar Bush as head of the newly created Office of Scientific Research and Development issued the foundational report *Science: The Endless Frontier*, which outlined why public funding of scientific research was beneficial and valuable for society:

> The Government should accept new responsibilities for promoting the flow of new scientific knowledge and the development of scientific talent in our youth. These responsibilities are the proper concern of the Government, for they vitally affect our health, our jobs, and our national security. It is in keeping also with basic United States policy that the Government should foster the opening of new frontiers and this is the modern way to do it. For many years the Government has wisely supported research in the agricultural colleges and the benefits have been great. The time has come when such support should be extended to other fields.
> (United States & Bush, 1945)

In addition to making the argument of the economic and societal benefits in sustained investment for basic research after the war effort, Bush called for the creation of a dedicated agency to manage and administer research. Bush's recommendation directly led to the creation of the National Science Foundation (NSF). Investment in scientific research in the immediate post-war period was an accepted good for national security and economic competition, but as resources for funding are no longer able to keep pace with research and innovation. Funding scarcity naturally led to increased scrutiny on the value of research and justification for continued funding. Satler and Martin (2001) categorized the economic benefits of publicly funded research as:

- Increasing the stock of useful knowledge.
- Training skilled graduates.
- Creating new scientific instrumentation and methodologies.
- Forming networks and stimulating social interaction.
- Increasing the capacity for scientific and technological problem-solving.
- Creating new firms.

It is notable that the focus on solving problems or improving existing systems is not one of their explicit benefits. Workforce development and fostering social cohesion through public knowledge do have economic benefits, but also clear societal benefits. Translating academic research to formats and venues that can be used by other parts of society is critical to ensure its relevance and thus give it a chance of having some impact outside the ivory tower. Nightingale and Scott (2007) suggest, "Funders need to recognize the distinction between relevance and academic impact." They go on to argue research that performs well according to traditional scholarly metrics might be good for an academic field but not society:

> Impact may be easy to measure and audit, but relevance is not. The way that the thing being measured by impact metrics is changed by being measured (game-playing and so on) calls into question the entire foundation of the assumed association between research quality and the disciplinary judgements of value that inform performance metrics. (Nightingale & Scott, 2007, p. 547)

This concern about gaming the metrics hints at another problem in the relationship be academic research and society – that it encourages researchers and funders to focus on areas that can be easily measured, often at the exclusion of less quantifiable research areas. Ernø-Kjølhede and Hansson (2011, p. 136) warn:

> the obvious danger is that researchers and universities intensify their efforts to participate in activities that can be directly documented rather than activities that are harder to document but in reality may be more useful to society.

Accountability and assessment are important parts of any research program and should be part of the standard practice, but it cannot be discounted (and should likely be addressed elsewhere) that the desire for easily quantifiable metrics is shaping the way research is approached and likely detrimental to certain lines of inquiry. Developments in this area reflect the contemporary neoliberal research environment at public universities (and the rest of the public sector): commodification and regulation (Burawoy, 2011). As a result of these pressures, the need and desire to show how research impacts and influences society is important, but there also needs to be an understanding of the roles and responsibilities of both sides. Watermeyer (2016, p. 202) distilled this important question about the focus on impact and regulation, and the actions of academics with the observation that academics and knowledge workers are "increasingly beholden to the strategic and technocratic frameworks" of research bodies and government funding agencies. Societal impact of research is important and good, and should be considered when making decisions about public funding of research activities. As models of assessment are developed though, the focus on measurement:

> should not come at the expense of basic, blue-sky research, given that it is and will remain near-impossible to predict the impact of certain research projects years or decades down the line. (Bornmann, 2012, p. 676)

One effort to assess the impact of research projects, and by extension research programs, is the Research Excellence Framework (REF). Developed in the United Kingdom by prominent higher education funding bodies in 2014 to create a shared policy aim for research assessment is to secure the continuation of a world-class, dynamic and responsive research base across the full academic spectrum within UK higher education (Higher Education Funding Council for England, 2018).

The REF provides accountability for public funding of research by producing evidence of the benefits of that investment, inform decision-makers in the allocation of research funding. The framework process includes expert reviews, systematically conducted by panels of academics and research users to assess the impact of research outputs outside academic settings (Higher Education Funding Council for England, 2018). During the REF 2014, 1,911 impact templates were assessed and graded by these review panels, with a total of 6,075 impact case studies (Manville et al., 2015). Developing and assessing the case studies and assembling the panels to do so were very resource intensive and costly for all involved. The REF 2014 was seen as a worthwhile and successful exercise, somewhat unexpected for an initial effort, and the buy-in from academics and research users was pivotal in the REF's success (Manville et al., 2015). Critiques of the REF question if this culture of assessment is in conflict with the traditional missions of universities, and that rewarding and encouraging entrepreneurial academics will likely have long-term effects not yet apparent, and the "overall impact of 'impact' on the academic community is thus too soon to calculate" (Watermeyer, 2016). If the REF is to really be successful and a culture of impact assessment is fully adopted by the UK academic research community, then there will also need to be dedicated resources (in funding and time) to make sure the initiative is not "tokenistic" (Parker & Teijlingen, 2012).

The United States had a similar project that was launched in 2010; STAR METRICS® (Science and Technology for America's Reinvestment Measuring the EffecTs of Research on Innovation, Competitiveness and Science) is a project from the National Institutes of Health and the NSF, under the auspices of the Office of Science and Technology (National Institutes of Health, 2019b). The project reflected the goals of the American Recovery and Reinvestment Act, the comprehensive federal stimulus bill focused on job creation, digital and physical infrastructure improvements, and increased government transparency and accountability. STAR METRICS® would look at the employment impacts of federally funded research, and then look at the broader impacts of federal scientific research along the following themes: economic growth, workforce outcomes, scientific knowledge, and social outcomes (NSF, 2019). Collecting data to assess the programmatic impacts was halted in 2016 though, and the project has shifted focus with the development of Federal RePORTER, a database which will normalize data about federal scientific research grants (National Institutes of Health, 2019a). There is still a demonstrated need for a national framework for assessing and communicating the impacts of research programs.

Transportation

In transportation, frequently the impacts can be distilled to time, lives, and money. Time is often used to demonstrate different measures of mobility, such as how many vehicles travel on a stretch of road during a period of time, the travel times for system users, or how many people ride a transit system. The 2012 transportation authorization bill, Moving Ahead for Progress in the 21st Century Act

(MAP-21) established a performance- and outcome-based program to ensure that transportation projects were accountable and furthered national transportation goals. The seven performance areas targeted in MAP-21 follow the "lives, money, and time" model but are more detailed across different aspects of the transportation system. They are:

- Safety.
- Infrastructure condition.
- Congestion reduction.
- System reliability.
- Freight movement and economic vitality.
- Environmental sustainability.
- Reduced project delivery delays (Federal Highways Administration, 2013).

These performance measures were strengthened in the following transportation authorization bill, Fixing America's Surface Transportation (FAST) Act, which shortened the deadlines for State departments of transportation and metropolitan planning organizations to meet their performance goals, and if a state fails to meet their freight performance goals, they must include actions to correct that in their reports (Federal Highways Administration, 2017). This culture of performance measurement has extended to outputs in the form of research programs (particularly those funded by federal and state agencies). Such areas of accountability are fundamental to those research programs.

The Environmental Protection Agency (EPA) uses 12 performance measures for evaluating sustainable transportation initiatives. They are similar to those laid out in MAP-21 but also go a bit farther to look at how transportation systems function and are planned. They are:

- Transit accessibility.
- Bicycle and pedestrian mode share.
- Vehicle miles traveled (VMT) per capita.
- Carbon intensity.
- Mixed land uses.
- Transportation affordability.
- Benefits by income group.
- Land consumption.
- Bicycle and pedestrian activity and safety.
- Bicycle and pedestrian level of service.
- Average vehicle occupancy.
- Transit productivity (US EPA, 2014).

These measures address transit and active transportation (cycling and walking) use and adoption, which is critical in sustainable transportation and reducing greenhouse gas emissions produced from transportation. Multimodal assessment is also necessary to evaluate the performance of the whole transportation system, since no mode operates in isolation from the others. The measures are also greatly influenced and largely determined by land-use patterns and other externalities. Ultimately though, they can be distilled to the same lives, time, and money.

The term "Level of Service" (LOS) is a key part of planning to communicate the impacts of a project on the system, although in 2013 California legislation (SB-743) was signed into law that largely did away with LOS requirements, in favor of people moved (Steinberg, 2013). Lives can crudely be distilled into safety terms of fatalities or injuries incurred while using the transportation system. Often this is a measurement of fatalities of road users, cyclists, pedestrians, or workers (such as highway maintenance or construction crews). Other public health measures, such as the impact on air quality for areas surrounding transportation facilities is also another up-and-coming metric for some transportation projects, though not widely adopted yet. Money as a metric takes on many forms, but also shows how focusing on economic impacts is a pragmatic approach to securing and maintaining funding for transportation programs. Some ways economic impact is measured include monitoring pavement quality (which has impacts on vehicle wear and emissions, but is also an indicator of pavement performance and potential lifecycle costs), travel times (as a reflection of economic performance and the external costs of congestion), and other cost benefits achieved through improved operations across all sectors in transportation (from maintenance to planning to administration).

There has been considerable work in communicating the value of transportation research to stakeholders that ultimately decide on funding and priorities, but the emphasis has largely been on government research programs. In 2009, the Transportation Research Board (TRB) published the guidebook *Communicating the Value of Transportation Research* (NCHRP Report 610) which gives a broad overview for agencies and research programs to demonstrate their value. It recommends that researchers "adopt a principle of continual communication as part of [the] research process" (National Cooperative Highway Research Program, 2009). It also stresses that communicating value is context specific, dependent upon the nature of the project, the desired outcomes, and the intended audience. While the guidebook is clearly intended for research administrators, those involved with technology transfer, and communications teams, their approach of context-focused case studies presents a good model. Particularly since many of these research programs have diversity in the scale, scope, and topics of projects, that cut across many of the performance areas described above. The anecdotal case study approach is more feasible in terms of tracking and describing to stakeholders even if it does not give a holistic view of a research program. There is also an added level of separation from transportation research programs at academic institutions, since the government agencies largely focus on their research outputs (technical reports) and ignore other research products, such as peer-reviewed articles or data. There is also a disconnect of attribution whereby the time a research project is completed and parts of it are implemented or deployed, frequently the original academic researchers are only mentioned in passing if at all. As a result, connecting academic research to the deployed research can be difficult and labor intensive.

The Institute of Transportation Studies

The ITS was formed in 1947 by the California State Legislature to perform research to shape the state's transportation needs. It was the first research institute of its kind established in the United States (though several soon followed in other states). As the state and the UC system grew, ITS evolved into a four-campus model with institutes at Berkeley, Davis, Irvine, and UCLA. Each campus performed distinct, and at times complementary (or competing), research projects. ITS funding has been allocated through the Public Transportation Account (PTA) of the state budget, but the total amount given to the campuses remained largely unchanged at $980,000 annually since the 1970s. In 2016, the four-campus ITS successfully appealed to Sacramento for a one-time funding increase across the system to $3 million. In the next fiscal year (2017–2018), continued funding was increased to $5.98 million across the system from revenues in the Road Maintenance and Rehabilitation Account generated from an increase to the state's gas tax (Senate Bill 1, or SB1) (UCOP, 2018). Due to California's peculiar ballot initiative process, this funding was not certain until Proposition 6 (which would have repealed the new increase in the gas tax) was defeated in November 2018 (Swan, 2018). Had Prop. 6 passed, most of the UC-ITS research and other efforts would have ceased immediately. Before the funding increases, most of the PTA money was allocated for administrative functions, such as programmatic staffing, research management, and the ITS Library at Berkeley. Funding for the different research centers and groups associated with ITS comes through grants and contracts from a variety of sources: Caltrans, the California Air Resources Board, United States Department of Transportation (USDOT), United State Department of Energy (USDOE), Environmental Protection Agency (EPA) private companies, and so on. The extra funding from PTA and now SB1 will support small-scale, exploratory research that directly addresses California's transportation needs. These projects will also provide some stable funding and support for graduate students, a common limiting factor in any graduate program.

Through the process of approaching Sacramento for increased funding, the need to demonstrate the value and impact of ITS research across the state was an explicit priority, following similar performance measurement expectations outlined in MAP-21 and the FAST Act. For some projects, such as the integrated corridor management system piloted in Connected Corridors, it was easy to demonstrate the effects of the research on the transportation system, such as a decrease in travel times along the corridors where the system was deployed (California PATH, 2018). Other research, such as looking at potential policies to encourage the adoption of zero-emission vehicles and effects that might have on greenhouse gas emissions, was much more difficult to quantify. When the four ITS directors went to Sacramento for increased funding, demonstrating the value of the programs was a necessity. As part of that effort, a comprehensive bibliography of research for each of the ITS campuses was compiled by the ITS librarian, including citations from Google Scholar. This crude method of demonstrating breadth and reach of ITS research illustrated the possibilities of using bibliometrics and other tools to quantify research outputs systematically. These metrics were then used to demonstrate value of the research programs to stakeholders and demonstrate that taxpayers' money was being used effectively to improve and innovate the state's transportation system. Using these metrics to illustrate the performance of the different ITS groups was both a show of accountability but also promotion – ITS research is used and respected.

The ITS Library was called upon to compile the bibliometric data after a similar exercise for an external academic program review at ITS Berkeley for the Vice Chancellor of Research in 2015. For that exercise, academic publications (articles, books, chapters, and conference papers) were compiled for all faculty and research staff from 2005 through 2015, which totaled about 1,000 items. Since the focus of that review was on the academic activities and output, non-academic publications, such as technical reports and white papers, were excluded. After collecting the publication data, it was evident that comparisons of research productivity across academic researchers through bibliometric indicators provided a limited view. It also must be acknowledged that publication output across different disciplines like the major engineering sub-disciplines varies, so directly comparing a civil engineer and an electrical engineer is like comparing apples to oranges (Lillquist & Green, 2010). As an example, the output of the computer science researchers at ITS Berkeley was more prolific yearly than some of the civil engineers, but the civil engineers were more likely to author technical reports for Caltrans or other state agencies, and these reports were not included in that citation set. The full collection of publications provided a broad overview of previous research activities of ITS Berkeley. Further, it provided a forensic view of successfully completed research for each of the research centers and faculty. Research thrusts, shifts in funding sources, and regular collaborators could be gleaned from looking at the bibliographic information.

The next iterations of the work, such as the bibliometric data compiled for the proposal to Sacramento for the increase in PTA funding, included gray literature in the publications set. This inclusion was especially important since many of those publications were reports for Caltrans, the California Air Resources Board, and other government agencies. Demonstrating that ITS research meets the needs of California and provides value to the state and others in the transportation community was a critical factor in the increase in PTA and SB1 funding. Although it was obvious there was room to improve tracking the results, impacts, and potential values of ITS research, how to do so was a lingering question – one that the research community has been working on for a while.

Tracking and Measuring Impact for ITS

After the initial collection of ITS Berkeley bibliographic data in 2015, the potential to use that data for programmatic assessment was evident. In transportation, like many other disciplines, the allure and impact of simple, straightforward metrics to show the efficacy or dysfunction of a system was powerful. The most well-known example in transportation was the Urban Mobility Scorecard from Texas Transportation Institute (n.d.), now the Global Traffic Scorecard from INRIX (n.d.), which provides clear rankings of traffic congestion in metropolitan areas. The data and methodologies used to generate the rankings never got as much attention as the simple measures that are frequently cited. Access Across America from the University of Minnesota's Center for Transportation Studies is another set of measures used to compare different transportation regions that is frequently referenced (Accessibility Observatory at the University of Minnesota, n.d.) (http://access.umn.edu/research/america/). Instead of traffic volumes, the series' focus is on the access to work, services, and housing through different transportation modes. Would it be possible to derive a similar set of metrics for transportation research? No. It would not be possible in any meaningful way because a more qualitative approach would be necessary. There have been attempts to establish some correlation between citations and research performance in transportation, but they rely on the scholarly metrics methods described above which only measure the performance of transportation researchers in a narrowly defined way (purely academic) (Hanssen & Jørgensen, 2014). This narrow approach does not reflect the full potential impacts of any given transportation research project. Other efforts to apply scientometrics to transportation research do not address the inherent limitations of the approach, such as the limited scope to academically published research. They can, however, be a useful approach to gain insights into network effects and trends in the academic transportation research community (Heilig & Voß, 2015). These techniques can be useful to analyze part of the performance of a transportation research program, but other tactics also need to be employed to include adoption either through practice or through policy.

Aside from the fact that it is inappropriate and reductive to compare different kinds of research projects with different outcomes and goals using a simplistic metric, the amount of work to collect the data to even attempt that kind of measurement is onerous and not sustainable. If the publications in question were only from academic venues, then tools like Web of Science or Scopus might be sufficient, but even then, that can be problematic for transportation research which is inherently interdisciplinary and cuts across the typical publishing ecosystems. This is another reason it is compelling to use Google Scholar citations as an indicator despite the unreliability of their data and uncertainty of methods. Research stakeholders are often pleased that Google Scholar citation numbers tend to be bigger and more impressive, even if the actual value is not explicitly clear. Taking a case studies approach to measuring the impact of research is a compelling idea, but also labor intensive. It requires an ethnographic approach to talking to researchers, stakeholders, and the end users to learn how the research products are consumed and used. Especially because much of this research is freely available online, it is unreasonable to ask anybody who might read a report, "Did you find this useful? How useful?" Looking at citation rates is a somewhat sufficient proxy for this metric, though it just shows something was regarded enough to be cited. The sentiment and the utility of the citation would still need to be evaluated on a case-by-case basis. This approach also assumes the citations are correct enough to be picked up by Google Scholar, which is far from guaranteed, and also requires the research to be cited or mentioned in works that are publicly available to be indexed by Google. For many agencies, technical memos and internal reports are only available to staff on an organizational intranet. In some areas of transportation research, where ultimately the real impact of the research comes from adoption or deployment in the field, attribution of that work in the field can be nearly impossible to track. The same is also true for public policy, where a policy recommendation might be written in response to a research project that makes a case for a certain change, but there will not likely be any citation of the research or consultants in the legislation or laws. One proposed framework for assessing the impact of social sector organizations (such as non-profits and non-governmental organizations) takes a context-sensitive approach that focuses on the scope and scale of an organization's mission and operations (Ebrahim & Rangan, 2014). The framework tracks outputs, outcomes, and impact as they fall on different geographic scales. This approach could be applied to UC-ITS research and other functions, to make sure the assessment methods match the actual scope and scale of the product.

Documenting PTA/SB1 Projects

When UC-ITS was spun up following the increase in core funding from Sacramento, it was an opportunity to incorporate tracking and measurement of completed research into the entire research process. From the outset, consideration for how deliverables can be improved and organized was built into the research administration process. Research managers were consulted about setting expectations of reporting and assessment to ensure that sentiments of the ITS directors and stakeholders in Sacramento were addressed. The importance of being able to demonstrate the reach and impact of these research activities was very clear. This approach builds upon the ideas of accountability and performance measurement that were core to MAP-21 and the FAST Act, which set the agenda for transportation in the United States. The ITS Library provided guidance in the initial discussions and planning of the administrative process, stressing the need for unique identifiers to track projects and their deliverables. Incorporating assessment from the inception of a project would generate a richer dataset that can lead to more meaningful insights and analysis. A broad overview of the process follows:

1. When projects are approved and vetted by UC-ITS leadership, they are entered into a master spreadsheet and assigned a project number. This number acts essentially as a contract number, with which all subsequent research products will be associated.
2. Relevant project information, such as preliminary investigators, campuses involved, budget and scope of the project, and anticipated deliverables are also included. Not all projects will result in publications. Some will result in meetings, workshops, or trainings, and will not have any final documentation. Other projects might result in an online resource or tool. For projects that will result in written publications, there is the expectation of at least two publications: a policy brief and a written report.
3. All policy briefs and reports are published on the UC-ITS eScholarship repository, rather than the individual websites of the campus performing the research. Standardized templates are used to give publications a uniform look and guaranteed that all required elements are included. Reports include a technical report documentation page using the Federal Highways Administration (FHWA)

template to present all of the project's information in the document. This is done to show the unified cooperation of UC-ITS but also to ensure there is only one version of the publication to be tracked and cited, making that process as simple as possible.
4. The project number is included on each publication to link it back to any other related works. Digital Object Identifiers, or DOIs are also assigned to each report, publication, and policy brief to make citation and attribution even easier. The reports are assigned report numbers that are mostly derived from the project number, but not always. This is done as yet another way to disambiguate reports and make it easier for others to cite and reference, following conventions of technical reports from many other agencies, like Caltrans and USDOT. These report numbers are often used for retrieval purposes in other systems and databases to which the reports are added.
5. When the project is completed and closed out, the record is updated. Report numbers, DOIs, and URLs to the reports and policy briefs are added to the record. Any projects with outstanding deliverables will be readily apparent.
6. Reports are indexed in TRB's transportation research database TRID, which is widely used by researchers and practitioners. It is also indexed by Google. (Both eScholarship and TRID are also found in Google Scholar searches.)

So far only the initial round of PTA-funded research has been completed and published, which has proven to be a good test of the publication process. Even though the technical publications are often an afterthought of the research process, by making it an explicit part of project management, the reports and policy briefs are worked into the research process. Making the expectations known from the outset and explicitly including all of the elements that will make tracking feasible reflects a change in culture: there is an understood need for research assessment by all involved. The policy briefs are a new publication format whose focus, as the name suggests, are on policies that could be derived from the research. They are two-page documents that summarize the research in a clear and digestible format, with figures that make the findings easy to understand. The briefs' intended audience are policymakers and advisors in Sacramento, who take some kind of action from the research findings, though the briefs are really for anybody interested in the area who might not have the time (or technical understanding) to read the full report.

Tracking PTS/SB1 Projects Now

With the system described above now operational, there is a decent foundation in place to assess any impacts of the UC-ITS research funded through PTA/SB1. While this proposed methodology is intrinsically based upon the situational needs and resources of UC-ITS, it is also meant to be applicable to other research programs. An eventual goal is to have this culture of research assessment adopted by all ITS researchers across the four campuses. These methods could also be adapted to meet organizational needs of other academic research centers whose work encompasses policy, practice, and society.

The metrics used to assess the impact of research reflect the priorities of the stakeholders, but also can be sustainably collected given limited resources and time. This context-sensitive approach will focus on the value and impact of projects on an individual basis, measuring the impact of the project against its stated goals. Comparing projects in aggregate will likely happen, but that is not the intended use of these metrics beyond broad statements about the value of transportation research.

Evaluation of individual projects relies on these areas:

- Citations and other references to policy briefs and reports in aggregate as pulled from Google Scholar
- Citations and references to PTA/SB1-funded research in the media and other popular sources
- Academic publications (journal articles or conference papers) derived from PTA/SB1-funded projects, and their scholarly metrics
- Adoption of the research in policy and practice
- Research that builds upon the projects funded by PTA/SB1

Collecting and tracking citations, although likely outside the traditional scholarly publishing system, remains the most easily quantifiable metric. Collection and tracking will be done semi-regularly during the year following a project's completion. Assessment of the citation data will not really be useful until five years after a project's completion, since that is a reasonable time scale to expect some kind of reception and adoption of the research beyond initial discussions. Using Google Scholar makes the most sense at this time for collecting the citation information, because the reports and policy briefs will likely be from technical sources in addition to scholarly sources.

Capturing the mention and discussion of UC-ITS research in the media is also an important component of potential impacts of the research, because it elevates the research to the citizens whose tax dollars paid for it. Web alerts to keep track of media mentions of UC-ITS researchers will be used to complement tracking links of the documents (either through the URL or through the DOI). This multi-pronged approach is necessary because it is exceedingly common for media articles to discuss research without actually linking to or fully citing the report or article, but writers usually will give attribution to the authors. Using altmetrics to also compile these links would be beneficial, but initial attempts have not been very successful. Preliminary attempts in using altmetrics data to describe the reach of some ITS research were not fruitful because gray literature is not really monitored by altmetrics tools.

Tracking academic publications that come out of the PTA/SB1-funded research is another important measure, to show how this research not only contributes back to society but also to the academy. This also accounts for the reality that research takes different formats for different audiences, and to have a holistic view of its impact, all formats need to be accounted for. Encouraging authors to credit UC-ITS (or SB1) for funding will make this easier to focus tracking efforts, but given the current scale of UC-ITS research staff this can reasonably be accomplished by tracking citations for publications beyond those funded by PTA/SB1.

Determining how these research projects are adopted in the field, either through policy, integration in technical documents, or deployment, is the most difficult area to measure, but also the most important. The field is where the real, practical impact on society takes place. It could be argued that media attention that changes the attitudes or practices of individuals also has impact in changing human behavior that is also difficult to track and measure. An ethnographic approach will be needed to fill the gaps that other quantitative and automated methods (searching, linking, and alerts) will not be able to adequately capture. Keeping track of UC-ITS activities in Sacramento (and other similar venues) will help prioritize what to track. Paying attention to proposed California legislation (such as SB1 and SB743) to identify legislative bills that incorporate policy recommendations from UC-ITS research will also be necessary. Evaluating the influence of UC-ITS for transportation practitioners will also be largely context specific. Following up with the researchers to see if they are aware of any adoption from their colleagues in the field is one way this information will be collected. Another way will be following developments and changes in relevant technical guidelines, from either the state or other jurisdictions within California. Most UC-ITS projects have a noted stakeholder associated with them, which will make it easier to target efforts in this area, but focus should not be limited to those stakeholders. Good ideas may be adopted by practitioner or agency. And while the focus will be on adoption within California since this research is funded by the state's gas tax, tracking adoption across borders will be important and necessary. Commercialization of research—through patents, the creation of start-ups, or some other kind of partnership with industry—is another area of impact that is not quite accounted for in this model. Commercialization could be folded into tracking policy or other forms of adoption of research products, but the information sources will be quite different as will the time scale.

Including research that builds upon these projects is also an important metric that is not usually captured by most traditional methods and looks at a time scale that is not immediate. Recognizing that research projects build upon one another and evolve is an important part of the process. It will be nearly impossible to give full attribution to these projects, particularly because passing instances or ideas might have profound implications for other research in ways not easily attributable. Another area to develop over time is the documentation of research project "families," in which related projects naturally build upon one another and are interrelated. Assessing projects in a way that leads to some basic classification will document these relationships in the institute's research portfolio, which will help support giving a longer view of research assessment than would be possible if we were to focus on individual projects alone. The value of an earlier research project might not be apparent until much later when a subsequent project is completed. Project family documentation also acknowledges that research, change, and progress is a process that builds upon itself. Measures to show the impact of the initial research would include subsequent projects, especially those not funded by SB1.

An assessment portfolio will be created for each project to collate all these metrics and make them available for the researchers and UC-ITS staff. This portfolio will also be an important mechanism to collect citations, mentions, and other documentation needed for these case studies to be developed over time. As mentioned earlier, while tracking citations and gathering the information should begin shortly after projects are completed, it must continue for years to gain a meaningful understanding of what impacts may actually come from that research. The projects and their impacts will be measured using criteria based on the performance measures outlined by USDOT and the EPA for transportation. Since there is considerable overlap between those two sets of measures, they can be streamlined a bit. A few other topics, including social equity are, not accounted for in those performance measures, and that are important to the mission of UC-ITS. These topics will be included in the future. The proposed measures to track, as makes sense for each project, fit the following thrusts:

- Safety
- Infrastructure condition
- Congestion reduction/traffic flow
- System reliability
- Freight and goods movement and economic vitality
- Environmental sustainability and impacts
- Reduced project delivery delays
- Mode share
- System performance across modes
- Accessibility
- VMT per capita
- Land use and real estate
- Transportation affordability
- Social equity

By using these categories to evaluate projects, it helps keep like with like. Making sure the outcomes are appropriate for the stated goals of a project is also important. Context-sensitive evaluation tempers any notions of going by raw numbers, in pursuit of the largest, most easily measured numbers that can be generated. These easily quantifiable metrics may be impressive but have no real value absent the proper context.

Other Considerations and Potential Next Steps

The outlined methodology above is meant to be practical for organizations of varying sizes to adopt and use. The process of data collection could be improved upon by using systems like CrossRef or ORCID for tracking research outputs. This methodology was also developed for the most part before the November 2018 election, when the UC-ITS funding situation was not entirely certain, so potential resources, like ORCID, for publication aggregation were not included. Many UC-ITS researchers have ORCIDs because they are mandated in the USDOT Public Access plan, though it is not entirely clear how widely they are used beyond required instances. As the UC-ITS publication system develops and more publications are made with DOIs and other persistent identifiers, CrossRef may become a useful tool in tracking output and citations, though we are not yet there.

Another area that should be folded into this process is data citation and publication. While there has been a lot of discussion and enthusiasm for opening data in transportation, publication of transportation research data is still not very common. One reason for this is the barriers to sharing due to the lack of infrastructure, though that will most likely change with more stable funding. The main obstacle is that current culture around data in transportation research does not really emphasize sharing or publishing the data used in research. Some reasons are due to data agreements and licenses with vendors, or the sensitive nature of the data, no real incentives exist to increase publication and sharing practices. As the culture changes, and data and reporte are treated as deliverables and research products, then citation and potential reuse of data generated in UC-ITS research will also need to be accounted for.

Quantifying workforce development is another measure that could be incorporated, but would likely require a very different approach. For projects that fund graduate or undergraduate students, including how many and which students are supported in the project records would be useful. Students eventually become practitioners in some form, and accounting for them in the assessment of a project can establish a clear relationship to workforce development. For projects that include workshops or some other kind of event, it would be useful to not only note the numbers of attendees but also which sectors they represent. Quantitatively tracking the outcomes of workshops or other public meetings will be difficult, particularly if there is not a publication accompanying the meeting. Tracking mentions of ITS could help uncover some continuations of ideas from these workshops. Further work and development of performance measures and methods for public engagement which goes beyond attendance numbers is needed.

As these projects are evaluated it is important to remind stakeholders that metrics are only part of the evaluative context, and that research outputs cannot be adequately reduced to a simple set of numbers. While numbers might be eye-catching and help wow the public, a measured approach of powerful anecdotes while collecting a robust dataset will be needed. This methodology is designed to be extendable to the entire ITS research portfolio, including projects from other funding sources. Ideally the process could be adapted to work with the individual research centers, so that their administrators can work with the ITS Library in the necessary documentation and preparation at the beginning of the research project to more readily be able to measure and track progress upon completion. However, that would be a cultural change and require an infrastructure and continuity that does not really exist at this time.

References

Accessibility Observatory at the University of Minnesota. (n.d.). Access across America. Retrieved from http://ao.umn.edu/research/america/index.html. Accessed on November 30, 2018.

Archambault, É., & Larivière, V. (2009). History of the journal impact factor: Contingencies and consequences. *Scientometrics*, *79*(3), 635–649. DOI:10.1007/s11192-007-2036-x

Auger, C. P. (1998). *Information sources in grey literature* (4th ed.). London: Bowker-Saur.

Banister, D. (2014). Where to start? *Transport Reviews*, *34*(1), 1–3. DOI:10.1080/01441647.2013.874131

Bornmann, L. (2012). Measuring the societal impact of research: Research is less and less assessed on scientific impact alone—We should aim to quantify the increasingly important contributions of science to society. *EMBO Reports*, *13*(8), 673–676. DOI:10.1038/embor.2012.99

Bornmann, L. (2013). What is societal impact of research and how can it be assessed? A literature survey. *Journal of the American Society for Information Science and Technology*, *64*(2), 217–233. DOI:10.1002/asi.22803

Bornmann, L. (2014). Do altmetrics point to the broader impact of research? An overview of benefits and disadvantages of altmetrics. *Journal of Informetrics*, *8*(4), 895–903. DOI:10.1016/j.joi.2014.09.005

Burawoy, M. (2011). Redefining the Public University: Global and national contexts. In J. Holmwood (Ed.), *A manifesto for the public university* (1st ed., pp. 27–41). London: Bloomsbury Academic. http://www.bloomsburycollections.com/book/a-manifesto-for-the-public-university/ch2-redefining-the-public-university/

California PATH. (2018). Connected corridors program. https://connected-corridors.berkeley.edu/.

Ebrahim, A., & Rangan, V. K. (2014). What impact? A framework for measuring the scale and scope of social performance. *California Management Review*, *56*(3), 118–141. DOI:10.1525/cmr.2014.56.3.118

Ernø-Kjølhede, E., & Hansson, F. (2011). Measuring research performance during a changing relationship between science and society. *Research Evaluation*, *20*(2), 131–143. DOI:10.3152/095820211X12941371876544

Falagas, M. E., Pitsouni, E. I., Malietzis, G. A., & Pappas, G. (2007). Comparison of PubMed, Scopus, Web of Science, and Google Scholar: Strengths and weaknesses. *The FASEB Journal*, *22*(2), 338–342. DOI:10.1096/fj.07-9492LSF

Federal Highway Administration. (n.d.). A summary of highway provisions – FAST Act. https://www.fhwa.dot.gov/fastact/summary.cfm.

Federal Highway Administration. (n.d.). MAP-21 - Fact Sheets - Performance Management. https://www.fhwa.dot.gov/map21/factsheets/pm.cfm

Haddaway, N. R., Collins, A. M., Coughlin, D., & Kirk, S. (2015). The role of Google Scholar in evidence reviews and its applicability to grey literature searching. *PLOS ONE*, *10*(9), e0138237. DOI:10.1371/journal.pone.0138237

Hanssen, T.-E. S., & Jørgensen, F. (2014). Citation counts in transportation research. *European Transport Research Review*, *6*(2), 205–212. DOI:10.1007/s12544-013-0122-0

Heilig, L., & Voß, S. (2015). A scientometric analysis of public transport research. *Journal of Public Transportation*, *18*(2), 111–141. DOI:10.5038/2375-0901.18.2.8

Higher Education Funding Council for England. (2018). What is the REF? – REF 2021. https://www.ref.ac.uk/about/what-is-the-ref/.

INRIX. (n.d.). INRIX global traffic scorecard. http://inrix.com/scorecard/.

Institute of Transportation Studies. (n.d.). https://escholarship.org/uc/ucits

Kochetkov, D. M. (2018). A correlation analysis of normalized indicators of citation. *Publications*, *6*(3), 39. DOI:10.3390/publications6030039

Korevaar, J. C. (1996). Validation of bibliometric indicators in the field of mathematics. *Scientometrics, 37*(1), 117–130. DOI:10.1007/BF02093488

Lawrence, A., Houghton, J. W., Thomas, J., & Weldon, P. (2014). *Where is the evidence: Realising the value of grey literature for public policy and practice*. Victoria, Australia: Swinburne Institute for Social Research. DOI:10.4225/50/5580B1E02DAF9

Lillquist, E., & Green, S. (2010). The discipline dependence of citation statistics. *Scientometrics, 84*(3), 749–762. DOI:10.1007/s11192-010-0162-3

Manville, C., Guthrie, S., Henham, M.-L., Garrod, B., Sousa, S., Kirtley, A., ... Ling, T. (2015). Assessing impact submissions for REF2014 [Product Page]. https://www.rand.org/pubs/research_reports/RR1032.html.

National Cooperative Highway Research Program, Transportation Research Board, & National Academies of Sciences, Engineering, and Medicine. (2009). *Communicating the value of research: Contractor's final report*. Washington, DC: Transportation Research Board. DOI:10.17226/23034

National Institutes of Health. (2019a). Federal RePORTER – Smart Search: Find federal agencies scientific awards data from this easy to use seamless search interface. https://federalreporter.nih.gov/.

National Institutes of Health. (2019b). STAR METRICS® – Home. https://www.starmetrics.nih.gov/.

Nightingale, P., & Scott, A. (2007). Peer review and the relevance gap: Ten suggestions for policy-makers. *Science and Public Policy, 34*(8), 543–553. DOI:10.3152/030234207X254396

NSF – National Science Foundation. (n.d.). STAR METRICS: New way to measure the impact of federally funded research. https://www.nsf.gov/news/news_summ.jsp?cntn_id=117042. January 3, 2019.

Parker, J., & Teijlingen, E. van. (2012). The research excellence framework (REF): Assessing the impact of social work research on society. *Practice, 24*(1), 41–52. DOI:10.1080/09503153.2011.647682

Salter, A. J., & Martin, B. R. (2001). The economic benefits of publicly funded basic research: A critical review. *Research Policy, 30*(3), 509–532. DOI:10.1016/S0048-7333(00)00091-3

Seglen, P. O. (1997). Why the impact factor of journals should not be used for evaluating research. *BMJ, 314*(7079), 497. DOI:10.1136/bmj.314.7079.497

Shotton, D. (2013). Publishing: Open citations. *Nature News, 502*(7471), 295. DOI:10.1038/502295a

Steinberg (2013). Environmental quality: Transit oriented infill projects, judicial review streamlining for environmental leadership development projects, and entertainment and sports center in the City of Sacramento. Pub. L. No. SB-743. https://leginfo.legislature.ca.gov/faces/billNavClient.xhtml?bill_id=201320140SB743

Swan, R. (2018). Prop. 6: Californians reject gas tax repeal measure – SFChronicle.com. *San Francisco Chronicle*, November 7. https://www.sfchronicle.com/politics/article/Prop-6-California-gas-tax-increase-holds-narrow-13369294.php

Taubes, G. (1993). Measure for measure in science. *Science, 260*(5110), 884–886. DOI:10.1126/science.8493516

Terämä, E., Smallman, M., Lock, S. J., Johnson, C., & Austwick, M. Z. (2016). Beyond academia – Interrogating research impact in the research excellence framework. *PLOS ONE, 11*(12), e0168533. DOI:10.1371/journal.pone.0168533

Texas Transportation Institute. (n.d.). Urban mobility scorecard – Urban mobility information. https://mobility.tamu.edu/ums/.

The PLoS Medicine Editors (2006). The impact factor game. *PLOS Medicine, 3*(6), e291. DOI:10.1371/journal.pmed.0030291

UC Institute of Transportation Studies (ITS) | UCOP. (2018). UC Institute of Transportation Studies (ITS). https://www.ucop.edu/research-graduate-studies/programs-and-initiatives/state-and-systemwide-research/transportation-initiative.html.

United States, & Bush, V. (1945). *Science, the endless frontier. A report to the President.* Washington, DC: U.S. Government Publishing Office. https://catalog.hathitrust.org/Record/001474927

University of California Institute of Transportation Studies. (n.d.). Institute of Transportation Studies Publications. https://escholarship.org/uc/ucits

US EPA, O. (2014, January 7). Guide to sustainable transportation performance measures [Reports and Assessments]. https://www.epa.gov/smartgrowth/guide-sustainable-transportation-performance-measures.

Wagner, C. S., & Alexander, J. (2013). Evaluating transformative research programmes: A case study of the NSF small grants for exploratory research programme. *Research Evaluation, 22*(3), 187–197. DOI:10.1093/reseval/rvt006

Watermeyer, R. (2016). Impact in the REF: Issues and obstacles. *Studies in Higher Education, 41*(2), 199–214. DOI:10.1080/03075079.2014.915303

Watermeyer, R., & Hedgecoe, A. (2016). Selling 'impact': Peer reviewer projections of what is needed and what counts in REF impact case studies. A retrospective analysis. *Journal of Education Policy, 31*(5), 651–665. DOI:10.1080/02680939.2016.1170885

Chapter 4

A Breath of Fresh Air: New Bibliometric Services at EPA-RTP Library

Anthony Holderied and Taylor Abernethy Johnson

Overview

The US Environmental Protection Agency's Library at Research Triangle Park (EPA-RTP), North Carolina, is a special library of the federal government located within the organization's largest research facility. In addition to being a repository for air-related research, staff assist agency scientists and engineers through the provision of both traditional and forward-looking library services. Though the EPA-RTP Library had been involved in occasional bibliometrics-related reference inquiries and projects, the idea for a formalized research impact product did not take shape until recently. In 2016, library staff embarked on a journey to develop bibliometric services capable of demonstrating the value of agency scientists' and engineers' contributions to the organization. Years of exploration and experimentation resulted in products that packaged data from citations, scientific databases, and alternative metrics tools, with graphical visualizations communicating a story of impact. Through first the creation of a career-centric profile and later an article-focused output, library staff have worked to establish themselves as partners in bibliometric analysis, with further plans to grow several of these individual deliverables into a suite of research impact services.

EPA Origins

The EPA is a federal agency of the United States government whose mission is to "protect human health and the environment" by developing and enforcing regulations that are based on environmental laws passed by Congress.

EPA was established as a response to public outcry over environmental concerns beginning with Rachel Carson's *Silent Spring*, published in 1962 (The Origins of EPA, n.d.). Her book helped draw national attention to the misuse of chemical pesticides and resulting harmful effects on human health and wildlife. A number of environmental crises soon thereafter, including the 1969 Cuyahoga river fire, continued to highlight a growing need for one, centralized federal regulatory body to address environmental concerns (EPA History, n.d.).

In early 1970, with concerns over air quality and contaminated water, among other problems facing the country, President Richard Nixon presented the House and Senate with a 37-point message outlining a plan to consolidate the many environmental responsibilities of the federal government under one agency (The Guardian: Origins of the EPA, 1992). The plan would give the new agency the capacity to conduct research on important pollutants, monitor the condition of the biological and physical environment, establish baselines for measuring the success of abatement efforts, set and enforce standards for air and water quality, provide guidance to industries seeking to minimize environmental impact of their activities, and support state and local agencies with assistance and training (The Origins of EPA, n.d.). Following a series of congressional hearings in the summer of 1970, Nixon's proposal and request for four billion dollars was approved. EPA Order 1110.2 was signed by the agency's first Administrator William Ruckelshaus on December 2, 1970, thus officially establishing the agency as the nation's guardian of the environment.

An Agency of Evolving Priorities

Some of the agency's key regulatory actions began early with the control and reduction of emissions from transportation sources. With the authority to regulate motor vehicle pollution under the Clean Air Act, EPA created new standards for minimizing pollutants such as hydrocarbons, carbon monoxide, and nitrogen oxide. The agency also crafted a set of health-based standards known as the "National Ambient Air Quality Standards" which sought to regulate six criteria pollutants commonly found in the nation's air. The first fuel efficiency standards were created in 1975 under the Corporate Average Fuel Economy or CAFE program (Milestones in U.S. EPA and Environmental History, n.d.).

In 1976, the agency created another key regulatory development with Resource Conservation and Recovery Act (RCRA), a framework for managing hazardous and non-hazardous solid waste. (Resource Conservation and Recovery Act (RCRA) Overview, n.d.). Also in 1976, Congress enacted the Toxic Substance Control Act, which gave EPA the authority to protect public health and the environment through controls on toxic chemicals that pose an unreasonable risk of injury. Beginning in 1980, the agency developed its Superfund program designed to help manage the cleanup of the nation's worst hazardous waste sites and respond to significant environmental emergencies. The agency evolved in the 1990s to develop the popular Energy Star program for encouraging voluntary energy efficiency, as well as the Brownfields program which provides grants and tools to local governments for the assessment and cleanup of previously developed urban land that is no longer in use due to contamination. Over time, EPA has also been granted the authority to regulate drinking water, protect citizens from radiation, and most recently, create programs aimed at promoting environmental justice (Milestones in U.S. EPA and Environmental History, n.d.).

Throughout its history, agency initiatives have been supported by the EPA Library Network, a collection of libraries that began serving the agencies described in President Nixon's Reorganization Plan in July of 1970 (U.S. EPA, 1994, para.1). EPA Order 1300.01 outlined the creation of an agency-wide library network "designed to support staff in the program and regional offices and provide them with access to environmental information and related scientific, technical, management, and policy information" (EPA Chief Information Officer, 2016, p. 1). As the agency evolved, the network evolved to adapt to changes in technology, information access, and policy needs.

EPA-RTP Library in Support of Research

Today, the library network supports agency work by providing resources and services to the regulatory, administrative, and scientific research personnel at 25 locations across the country. Some libraries exist to support a specialized area of research such as watershed ecology, while others emphasize support for legal work being done at the agency. The three largest EPA libraries in Washington D.C., Cincinnati, and RTP, North Carolina, are designated repositories, meaning they house permanent physical collections of EPA reports and documents. These libraries also provide a full range of services, as they have larger staffs, while some of the more specialized libraries are run by solo librarians.

Although headquartered in Washington, D.C., EPA's footprint in RTP represents its largest facility and is home to over 2,000 employees. The RTP campus covers more than one million square feet and comprises 15 distinct offices, eight of which are research related. Much of the emphasis on scientific research at RTP is focused on air pollution and regulatory development related to the Clean Air Act and its associated National Ambient Air Quality Standards. The primary research organizations that reside within the RTP campus fall under the Office of Research and Development (ORD) and the Office of Air and Radiation. There are numerous research divisions within ORD that the library actively supports. Among the largest include the National Exposure Research Laboratory, the National Health and Environmental Effects Research Laboratory, the National Center for Computational Toxicology, and the National Risk Management Research Laboratory. Together, these labs and centers produce the bulk of original internal and extramural research produced by the agency. Some of the major research programs at EPA are carried out through these offices including air and energy research, chemical safety, human health risk assessment, homeland security research, sustainable water resources, and healthy communities research.

The EPA-RTP Library has been staffed by contractors through the University of North Carolina at Chapel Hill's School of Information and Library Science since 1974 and supports the work of scientists and regulatory personnel committed to these research programs. The library is a major research and repository library within the network, whose mission is to provide a broad range of information support services to enable the research, standards setting, and administrative personnel of EPA/RTP to spend their time using information rather than searching for it.

In pursuit of fulfilling this mission, the EPA-RTP Library provides a wide range of traditional services to its constituents including interlibrary loan, reference, literature searching, instruction, publication assistance, and citation management support. Librarians support the research initiatives of campus staff by providing access to over 1,000 journals, 6,000 books, and 13,000 scientific reports, while obtaining over 10,000 articles, documents, and standards from other libraries for its patrons each year. Staff provide bibliographic instruction and tutorials on the use of information tools and scholarly publishing topics, while also serving as the campus authority on utilizing EndNote for citation management. A key aspect of the library's suite of services is research assistance. For decades, librarians have worked side by side with scientists to develop complex search strategies and execute expert literature searches to aid in literature reviews, update industry technology standards, and conduct policy-related research.

Librarians work with scientists and regulatory personnel to provide information that is used to create models, develop assessments, set pollution standards, assist in publishing endeavors, inform policy, and discover how agency research is used around the world. Across the research offices, librarians support scientists by locating literature pertaining to toxicity of environmental substances and the resulting impacts on human health. Examples of these projects include research on emissions from animal production facilities, effectiveness of air pollution control technologies, methods of decontaminating anthrax in public spaces, and measures of the health effects of human exposure to artificial sports fields. Librarians also assist policy staff in a number of ways. In addition to finding the most recent regulatory information pertaining to an EPA rule, staff regularly provide literature that supports Risk and Technology Reviews (RTRs). These RTRs are required of the agency under the Clean Air Act (CAA) and are conducted by EPA personnel on an ongoing periodic basis to ensure the most effective means of controlling emissions in a particular industry process are employed. Examples of industries included in the CAA compliance are roofing manufacturing, oil and natural gas production, pharmaceuticals, polymers and resins, shipbuilding, metal furniture, and dozens more.

Bibliometrics at EPA

Bibliometric Requests

The EPA-RTP Library's most recently added research service began its development during early 2016, as librarians recognized a need for researchers to have current information and data pertaining to the research impact of the scholarship produced by themselves and their colleagues. Its foray into developing "Research Impact Services," however, started more recently and evolved slowly from humble beginnings. Historically, the EPA-RTP Library has provided research impact services without formally stating such by answering quick metrics-related reference questions, conducting extended publication tracking projects, providing impact-related instruction topics, and collaborating with researchers on large-scale bibliometrics gathering endeavors. Reference transactions were generally completed in response to data-gathering efforts needed for awards and performance evaluation submissions, typically filled using the library's subscription to the Web of Science suite. One major scientific achievement award granted to individual scientists annually by the agency requires journal-level metrics for each submitted publication, including Impact Factor, Immediacy Index, and Cited Half-Life. These metrics are gathered per individual request and can be quickly retrieved from Journal Citation Reports (JCR). Sometimes requests expanded to include author-level metrics such as h-index or citation counts for all of an individual's publications. Processes for filling these requests were not uniform, but typically involved an export of data from Web of Science and manual entry from JCR. This information was put into either an Excel spreadsheet or Word document and emailed to the patron, and was mostly numerical or tabular in nature. When necessary, the library supplemented analyses conducted using Web of Science with data from free tools such as Google Scholar. As inquiries pertaining to these resources increased with frequency, formal and informal trainings were provided by staff ranging from at-the-desk assistance with Web of Science and JCR to instruction sessions introducing bibliometric-related topics and usage of new tools for analysis such as Altmetric, Impact Story, and Plum Analytics.

During this earlier "era" of bibliometrics assistance, it was often difficult to gauge the interest and intention of use for bibliometric data among research staff at EPA-RTP, although librarians understood that a likely driver of this increase in bibliometric interest resulted from external funding pressures placed on individual research units to justify the existence of certain programs and products. Interactions with top-level administration in the past have been somewhat limited in terms of how this information can and should be used. Much of the information library staff have had on how metrics were valued within the organization was either speculative, or perceived based on anecdotal evidence from researchers and management. As popularity of research impact as a topic and the library's ability to provide services grew, opportunities arose for larger projects and partnerships with teams of researchers and programs. In one project, the library gathered bibliometric data including Journal Impact Factors and citation data for over 1,000 publications produced by one group. For another division, library staff worked on a time-consuming endeavor to produce publication and citation alerts in Web of Science for a large list of authors. Both of these projects went beyond the time and effort typically required for a reference interaction but were substantial learning opportunities for the library. Even though it was not always apparent to librarians the scope for which the data would be used, these projects in conjunction with the growing number of smaller bibliometrics requests began to demonstrate that a clear need for bibliometric data existed, making the library an obvious source for gathering metrics and informing researchers about collection tools and methods.

Evolving Needs and Assessing Resources

In response to the early bibliometrics requests, library staff began to explore research impact and engage in conversations with other library community groups. Staff examined the literature and attended webinars and conference sessions about bibliometric services and data visualization. Guidance was sought in areas of design and metrics selection (Few, 2005; Roemer & Borchardt, 2015). In professional development groups and networking endeavors, staff gathered experiences from other librarians, and connected with targeted local colleagues and influential professionals in the field to help inform potential strategies. Over time as the information need was solidified, the idea for developing a more methodical research impact product was established.

Through these connections with other libraries and the research impact community, staff gained a clearer picture of the types of deliverables and services other libraries were offering their patrons. While some of these products required resources and training the library did not have, there were certain aspects the library would be capable of providing. The library had several valuable subscription-based tools and a number of freely available resources at its disposal, which staff were already using to answer basic impact inquiries. These resources could immediately be used to develop the foundation of a formalized research impact product. For example:

- Extracting Web of Science data
- Using the data to create visualizations
- Collecting freely available Altmetric data

Information from these sources and tools could be pulled together into an organized, attractive report. After learning of a freely available tool for procuring Google Scholar data, Publish or Perish, the library had the beginnings of a structured research impact product using resources already available to them.

Web of Science. A subscription to Clarivate Analytics' Web of Science has provided the data foundation for answering bibliometrics questions. The discovery of the Citation Report and Analyze features were key in kindling ideas for research impact products, and deeper data investigation was fostered through the acquisition of *InCites*. Though gaps in coverage and a steeper learning curve are recognized weaknesses of these tools, their bibliometric data comprise the backbone of the library's research impact product prototyping. Staff were already familiar with the Web of Science database as a tool for searching, so learning the bibliometric analysis tools was the next step. *InCites* has proven to be more challenging with its frequently changing interface and without the previously established familiarity. As mentioned, JCR was regularly consulted to gather journal-level metrics. Throughout the development of different research impact projects and through many interface updates, library staff continue to use JCR to gather information about journal rankings, but the majority of data needed in the reports were integrated into the *InCites* platform. The workflow generally consists of creating a marked list in Web of Science and exporting the marked list as an *InCites* dataset. The Analyze feature of JCR is then used to supplement certain metrics.

Publish or Perish. To complement Web of Science data and attempt to fill some of the coverage gaps, library staff employed Publish or Perish, a free software utilizing Google Scholar citation data. Library staff began creating document lists in Publish or Perish and then harvesting the Google Scholar data directly into Excel spreadsheets, without the need for manual entry or exports to reference managers. While users must be careful in cleaning the data to ensure only the target author or articles are being exported, the streamlined citation gathering helps to expand results beyond what is available in Web of Science. The database also instantaneously provides several research impact indicators such as h-index, g-index, total citations, and average citations per paper. Through recent version updates, the library has been able to implement Publish or Perish when investigating gray literature. While Google Scholar's broad data scope opens the library's analysis capabilities, users must be aware of the challenges with indexing, metric quality, and other factors associated with such a broad database (Halevi, Moed, & Bar-Ilan, 2017).

Altmetric Explorer. Early in the research process on bibliometrics, it was clear that alternative metrics were gaining popularity and the library would need to find a systematic way to capture them for incorporation into any sort of research impact product. A third and later addition to the library's research impact resource toolbox was the Altmetric Explorer. This database allowed staff to search a group of DOIs at the same time and extract attention data without having to examine the Altmetric page for each individual article. Depending on the article, a broad spectrum of metrics can be gathered including social media mentions, patent citations, references in policy documents, and mentions in news articles. The database has experienced extensive updates since the library first started using it and now encompasses a staggering number of outputs and attention sources with functionality growing quarterly.

Product Development

Research Impact Report

In January 2016, the library began prototyping the assembly of what would become a research impact report, or RIR. The report's foundation stemmed from a set of publications by a test author. From that group of publications, a dataset could be curated in Web of Science and Publish or Perish and from there, analyses of article-, author-, and journal-level metrics conducted. Selecting metrics required balancing what researchers had commonly asked for in reference interactions with examples from both historical measures of productivity and cutting-edge indicators which may be new to agency researchers (Kostoff, 1996; Butler et al., 2017). Each of these components were added to an Excel spreadsheet and developed into either a table or simple, single-color bar graph. These figures were pulled into a Word document, producing a concise, report-style deliverable.

An RIR assesses an author's publication history and career impact through the lenses of outputs, citations, co-authorships, research areas, funding sources, and journals in which publications appeared. The reports pair data with graphical illustrations in an attempt to summarize the researcher's body of work. Special attention is given to journal metrics as they are the most popular statistics sought in bibliometrics requests. Graphics, key performance indicators, and badges are utilized from several sources including Web of Science, Altmetric, and Google Scholar. In addition to using data visualizations to show relationships among the different areas of analysis, certain sections of the report try to highlight the author's most influential work. A sample RIR detailing metrics and graphics is provided in Appendix 1.

Library staff presented this deliverable at various local and virtual conferences in order to solicit feedback from librarian and information colleagues. A "soft" rollout was conducted by sharing the prototype with a number of agency researchers. As this was an evolving product, multiple components were revised and amended prior to the official release as a result of feedback and to align the reports more closely to the way advancement occurs within the division. The final product was officially rolled out in 2016, first being promoted at the library's annual open house event in April. Later in September, library staff conducted a webinar entitled "Measuring Your Research Impact," which provided an overview of bibliometrics and integrated the promotion of RIRs as a new library service. As a result of the class, the first two reports were requested by campus researchers, enabling new insights to be discovered by librarians as these "official" reports were developed over the next couple of months.

Throughout the creation of around two dozen reports that were requested and completed over the course of a year, several modifications to the template were made in order to accommodate patron requests and capture unique publication histories. For example, entire graphics are now dedicated to citations of EPA documents and patent citations, neither of which are easily captured by Web of Science analysis. While the report currently ends somewhat abruptly, an About this Report page is planned for future templates. This page would appropriately respond to feedback received about the metrics used in the report and the sources for different data pieces which have been directly implemented into the Agency's research evaluation process.

RIR-specific Challenges. In addition to the challenges of keeping the documentation current, several other constraints played a role in making RIR strenuous to produce (Fig. 1). First, the time required to create the dataset was highly variable depending on the career status of the requestor. Initially, it seemed plausible to conduct an author search with an advanced search string and varying filters. But then librarians started to realize how name disambiguation can influence the time equation. Through trial and error, the library has transitioned to a model where a CV or publications list is the primary starting point for any research impact product, as opposed to conducting a labor-intensive author search for the publications. This solution has proven to be highly beneficial when working on larger projects for teams and groups. Additionally, the career length of a researcher greatly influences a report's breadth. While an RIR

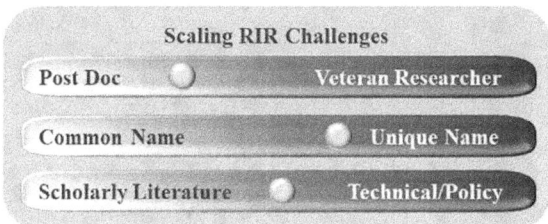

Fig. 1: The Spectra of RIR complexity are dependent upon the individual requestor and the nature of his or her publications

could be particularly useful for a postdoctoral student, it was typically found in practice that enough data could not be generated to populate a report. Lastly, only a number of divisions within the agency demonstrate productivity in the form of peer-reviewed research articles. Internal reports, technical documents, conference papers and abstracts, patents, and software are all documented and celebrated outputs that unfortunately lack many of the accepted bibliometrics indicators of journal articles. Over time, staff have experimented with manually calculating and creating graphics based upon CV data or other methods of research such as patent searching (Fig. 2). For these reasons and more, the RIR is a constantly evolving product.

The Next Cycle of Ideation

After almost a year of creating RIRs for patrons, the library reached a plateau in requests for the report after having completed reports for many of the library early-adopters who would be able to make use of one. Staff began discussing possibilities for expansion and what shape the next phase of research impact services could take for the library. It was acknowledged that RIRs were very time consuming and until a solution for automating the data extraction was available, such as employing the Web of Science Application Programming Interface (API), making a research impact product that was bigger in scale than an RIR would remain out-of-reach. It was also becoming evident that an author-centric model was applicable only in a few specific situations, such as with a promotion. Staff began to think about how productivity assessment occurred within the agency and what type of deliverable would align with that evaluation. Very rarely were careers examined and tracked, but productivity in the form of outputs was monitored on a regular basis. Entire internal systems and databases were constructed for the sole purpose of tracking publications from agency researchers. The library began to investigate how they could add value to this process.

Since expanding the scope was not possible with the current resources, staff began to prototype what a deep dive into a single output would look like. Closely examining the example provided by Makar, Malinowski, and Bhat (2017), the librarians developed prototypes for an Article Impact Report, or AIR, a deliverable that aims to assess the attention garnered by a single article authored by an EPA researcher.

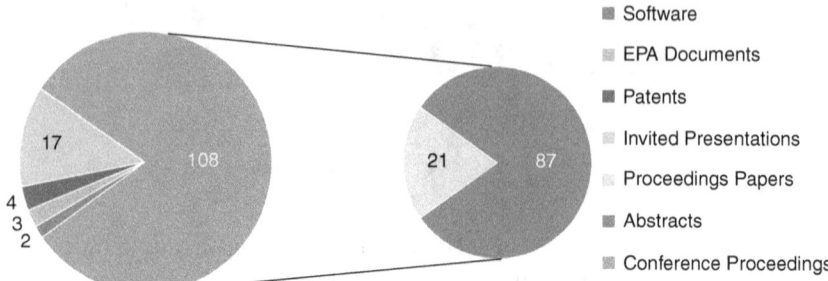

Fig. 2: Example graphic summarizing non-journal article publications

Article Impact Report

The template for an AIR was created with the RIR challenges in mind. The report was deliberately shorter, offering fewer graphics and less text which hopefully resulted in a shorter production time. The data visualizations for an AIR are primarily derived from Web of Science data and focus on the countries, organizations, journals, and research areas citing the target article. Altmetric tools assist in locating notable mentions and citations beyond scholarly literature. Other graphics and highlights are the result of unsystematically synthesizing information from different databases and manually searching the web. Article visibility and data availability is highly variable based on the subject matter, publisher, and individual author promotion. Examples of two AIRs can be found in Appendices 2 and 3. Aside from the scope, one major difference between the AIR and the RIR is how the AIR concludes with an "About this Report" section where a definition and data sources for each graphic are provided along with a small glossary for the altmetrics section. This addition came later and was based upon feedback from RIR service recipients. There are plans to add such a page for the RIR product in the future.

The rollout for AIRs closely mimicked that of RIRs. A few test reports were sent to patrons for feedback in early 2018. Later, another webinar about bibliometrics was developed and conducted in October 2018, integrating promotion of AIRs as the library's newest service. A formalized marketing campaign for AIRs is planned for 2019.

AIR-specific Challenges. The greatest challenge in AIR construction comes from the variability in accessible article data. The graphics and citation figures are highly dependent upon Web of Science data. The altmetrics page relies on the article being notably represented by either Altmetric or PlumX, and then receiving mentions somewhere. The best case scenario for producing a substantive AIR is when both types of metrics are present and can be gathered to sufficiently populate a report. When either one or both of the data components are missing, it becomes a labor-intensive forage across the web to extract enough relevant information to compile a report. This is especially true when examining non-journal article documents produced by agency researchers, as will be discussed later. Strategic searching for data "stand-ins" for these odd publications has resulted in counts of references found manually in the gray literature, displays of journal metrics, or even mini-AIRs (Appendix 4). For a mini-AIR, staff creatively use icons, colors, and space to produce a professional, innovative infographic for patrons that can fill some of the void left by absence of meaningful metrics derived from journal articles. Different iterations of this product are planned for 2019.

Discussion

Challenges

Aside from the report-specific challenges, the journey to create research impact products has required almost constant balancing and reassessment of time and resources. In addition to the time and training required to create the reports, it takes effort to stay informed of emerging technologies and assess their usefulness in the reports. These and other compromises are illustrated in Fig. 3.

One of the most time-consuming components of the entire operation was creating sufficient documentation so that the report production process could be replicated by a rotating cast of library staff that may be called upon to produce a report. Initially, the concern was getting the staff member familiarized with the field or "language" of bibliometrics, and the tools that are used to gather data. From there, the expectation is that the creator can follow a detailed guide that walks each staff person through the use of a template. The goal at the onset of creating the RIR as a product offering was to have step-by-step instructions for creating the report detailing how to export the data, create each component in Excel, then copy and paste the graphic or information into the template. Having such explicit instructions was complicated by the frequently shifting interface and database updates that would require retraining and updating guidance materials.

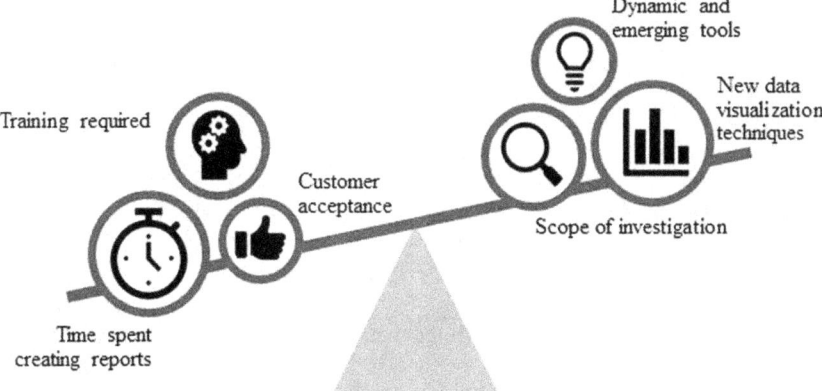

Fig. 3: Balancing organizational and operational considerations in research impact service development

As the tools continue to change and the menu of research impact products grows, keeping the guidance material up-to-date becomes more difficult. As staff become more experienced with making reports, it is more and more evident how different one report is from another. Trying to incorporate each and every unique graphic added per a researcher's request into the instructions would be overwhelming. So far, it is proving more time appropriate to use the documentation as a skeleton and remain flexible in letting the data reveal which areas of a report may require extra creativity.

Both RIRs and AIRs presented clear challenges in relation to staff resources. It is virtually impossible to know at the onset of either project if it will land on the lower or higher end of the labor spectrum. Many factors such as author name commonality, career length, and whether or not the author publishes primarily in the scholarly or gray literature could greatly influence the number of hours involved in creating a report. The library has been careful to monitor the scope of reports and ensure deadline expectations on the behalf of patrons are clear from the beginning. While the process can be slow for the first few reports, it becomes easier for the staff person as more reports are produced. Additionally as referenced earlier, the library has moved away from using author searching as a way to gather references and almost exclusively works from a CV.

Lastly, the data extraction process is highly laborious using basic .csv and .txt file exports. There is a significant amount of copying and pasting, importing external data, and formatting to get the data from the search results to the spreadsheet where it can be analyzed. While synthesizing the information from multiple databases is part of what makes the RIR and AIR unique from any other library service, it is acknowledged that streamlining is possible through automation. A goal that the library is taking steps to reach currently is to hire an intern with information science skills who can learn to work with APIs and incorporate them into the workflow to save time.

Biases and Limitations

The agency has recently placed an emphasis on using metrics to indicate evidence of mission support and goal success, particularly those which communicate impact as opposed to inputs and outputs. Librarians have been searching for their own methods of demonstrating value to the organization such as translating minutes spent serving patrons into researcher time saved, and possibly dollars saved. But finding understandable metrics to describe the impact of scholarly activities has been harder to define and develop into a service that patrons will find relevant and pertinent. As with any new service a library can offer, patrons must find applicable value in the product in order to see the product as a "need to have" instead of a "nice to have." Therefore, the library has tried to align the data components of the reports with the metrics agency researchers are interested in, while balancing the inclusion of new or unfamiliar metrics showing promise in the scientific field or library community in order to keep the reports on the leading edge. One example is the previously discussed Journal Impact Factor required for agency awards. While the library community and other stakeholders have acknowledged its weaknesses with regard to research impact evaluation, it is still, without fail the most-requested metric by agency researchers. So while these data must be included in the reports, if not serve as the key highlight for certain aspects, the library does its best to educate users on some of the up-and-coming metrics that can supplement the Journal Impact Factor whenever possible. Currently, this means incorporating several journal-level metrics, but normalized indicators, such as Journal Normalized Citation Impact, are gaining credibility in the literature and are candidates for inclusion in future requests. A complete list of metrics included in the library's research impact products, organized by metric level, is provided in Table 1.

Consistently, patrons who are learning about research impact metrics have emphasized the desire for a single, all-encompassing number. While such an indicator may be available in the future, the best solution bibliometrics librarians have been able to offer so far is a product that summarizes the leading metrics within one deliverable. For library staff, this type of product attempts to balance the biases and limitations of each data resource. Access to databases capable of

Table 1: Bibliometric indicators present across research and AIRs, categorized by level

Author	Article	Journal
Articles published per year	Citation counts	Impact factor
Career coauthoring institutions	Altmetric attention score	JCR category
Citations per year	Web of Science badges earned	Journal rank in JCR category
Funding agency support	Citations per year	Five-year impact factor
Items published	Top citing journal	Immediacy index
Research area participation	Social media mentions	Cited half life
Top journals published in	Reference manager captures	Article influence
Average citations per paper	Citations in news articles, patents, or policy documents	Eigenfactor
Total citations	Citations by country	
Percent cited papers	Citations by research area	
h-Index	Citations by organization	
g-Index	Citations by source title	
Citing articles (with and without self-cites)		

analyzing citation data is limited to Web of Science. Working with the database through its interface changes, system updates, and rocky implementation of new features has been difficult. As a supplement, the library works with other free tools such as Publish or Perish, a resource with its own set of limitations, and Altmetric, a tool that often requires an introduction for new users.

The analysis capabilities of altmetrics tools continue to gain ground as these platforms are developing valuable features seemingly daily. The biggest obstacle here has been encouraging researchers to trust and adopt Altmetric Attention Scores and PlumPrints as legitimate indicators of research impact. The current strategy is to emphasize the process behind the algorithms and be transparent about the strengths and weaknesses of each. Concurrently, promotion of how the tools reach into the gray literature and education on the importance of diversity in data sources helps staff encourage researchers to stay on the cutting edge.

One challenge the library has yet to find a comprehensive solution for is the abundance of gray literature produced within the agency. This material is rarely indexed in scientific databases or picked up by altmetrics. Consequently, the library has had to find creative ways to fill space when researchers' publications are primarily EPA or policy documents, or they want to highlight one particular policy document. Citation data can be found by manually searching the Internet, but there has yet to be a tool that saves time during this part of the process.

In trying to find solutions to this and other encountered obstacles, library staff are always on the lookout for new tools that can streamline different processes or provide insight in an area in which the current analysis is lacking. The conundrum then becomes whether or not staff have the time and bandwidth to learn the tool, especially if it requires advanced technical skills. Recently, the library converted one of its traditional internship positions into a position earmarked for an information science student. It is hoped that this student will be able to contribute to the research impact products by working with the recently produced APIs for Web of Science and Altmetric or possibly even learn Sci2, a network analysis program. Gaining technical knowledge would both streamline the report creation process to save time and open up possibilities for the library to provide research impact products on a larger scale.

Future Outlook

An unintended, yet serendipitous consequence of creating research impact services has been the increase in opportunities for staff to collaborate with research teams and divisions. The services have thus far been primarily marketed by word-of-mouth from one researcher to another. But recently, the library's outputs are making their way to organizational leaders who are excited to learn of the library's expertise with this genre of information. Team leaders and division directors are then asking how the library can be a partner in large, long-term metric-gathering endeavors, or to directly contribute to their internal processes for promotion and evaluation. Based on one recent project request of this nature, librarians at RTP have discovered that research offices within the agency report on scientific contributions and achievements through different mechanisms; that is, there is seemingly no uniform format for reporting year-end achievement across the divisions. For example, one of the divisions in the ORD produces year-end publications that are designed to be presented to management in order to highlight overall production and research achievement of the unit. Included in these products is a large poster that is displayed in the work area and a distributable annual report of 15–20 pages. The poster contains several graphical illustrations that represent the division's scientific accomplishments for the year. One graphic illustrates the number of peer-reviewed articles and other publications produced by type and sub-category. Another displays winners of honors and awards at the division, office, and agency level. The rest relate to specific products and deliverables developed by staff, which do not contain any associated metrics. The annual report contains only a short section of three pages that describe items with associated metrics. This section entitled "Production" lists the total number of unique, peer-reviewed journal articles and the number of journals in which the articles are published. There is also reference to the mean Journal Impact Factor of the group of papers and number of "first authors" listed. It goes on to list other types of publications produced by the group and some commentary on presentations delivered at various conferences and workshops around the world. From examples like these librarians discovered that metrics played a limited role in how an office presents its scientific research accomplishments. This in turn opens up the possibility for librarians to work with management to incorporate more substantive metrics and meaning into its reporting. It also helps continue to strengthen the position that the library has in being seen as an authority on demonstrating the value of research.

Going forward, the library is exploring variations on the RIR and AIR to begin to build a menu of research impact products for researchers to choose from in instances where the previously developed products do not directly support the need expressed by the patron. So far, the focus has been on a single researcher or article. Expanding the scope to encompass a team of authors or the totality of papers produced as the result of a single funding source, would better align the service with the method that research impact is assessed within the organization. Another example of future expansion would be tracking the global use or citation of a method or model developed by EPA scientists. Tools of this type such as BenMAP (Environmental Benefits Mapping and Analysis Program) are developed frequently by EPA and tend to attract high degrees of international attention and application. Growing research impact services in this way would provide EPA managers with another "story" for demonstrating value of research produced by one's division. These endeavors would most likely require more technical knowledge and additional tools capable of analyzing and visualizing tens of thousands of references, and possibly the use of a system with greater capabilities than Microsoft Excel.

Currently, the library does not have the resources to expand research impact services in ways that require advanced technical skills or expensive tools. But the library does have the benefit of a flourishing internship program bringing bright students who may possess certain software expertise or backgrounds in other useful areas such as marketing, programming, or graphic design. The library can also rely on interactions with patrons for feedback and insight into what metrics are most useful for them. Staff can then support those insights with the ever-growing body of literature surrounding alternatives and solutions to the widely used but reluctantly accepted measures of productivity and impact like the h-index.

More abstractly, the direction of research impact services will continue to be shaped from the requirements that organizational leaders place on researchers for promotion and evaluation. As an example, the library was recently asked to provide RIRs for candidates vying for an important vacancy within the division. Librarians have also been asked to provide data and narrative for how EPA policy has been viewed or mentioned in the news media. Other patrons have asked for assistance in creation of visualizations that can help make a case for continued funding of a certain program or technological tool developed within the agency.

Staff will likely continue to learn of these organizational requirements through information requests and invitations to collaborate on projects. As the library attempts to balance requests for traditional metrics like the Journal Impact Factor with new and alternative metrics, stakeholders will almost certainly be on the lookout for the best metrics to reflect the research impact of their work. Whether that focus will be on metrics of productivity, visibility, or attention, the researchers' requests and guidance provided by management will likely inform the future of research impact products developed within the library.

Conclusion

Having started the process of exploring and testing the potential for offering bibliometric services at EPA-RTP Library over two years ago, librarians have a good grasp of what has worked well and what improvements can be made to make the services more useful and attractive to RTP personnel. Librarians have made a number of significant changes to research impact products and processes over this time. Most notably, an additional deliverable (AIRs) was created to supplement the RIR in order to offer a product that is not only less time intensive to create, but adds a dimension that aims to demonstrate impact of a single contribution when a picture of the entire body of scholarship is not desired. This also serves the purposes of administrators who are interested in highlighting key contributions of a team without capturing the overall impact of the entire team's contributions. Products like these on the individual level and future planned expansions for teams and projects could become key in increasing the visibility of work conducted at RTP. To complement this work, library staff will continue to experiment and explore ways to help support the library's mission and propel researchers' efforts to demonstrate and communicate their value to the organization.

References

Butler, J., Kaye, D., Sebastian, A., Wagner, S., Morrissey, P., Schroeder, G., ... Vaccaro, A. (2017). The evolution of current research impact metrics from bibliometrics to altmetrics. *Clinical Spine Surgery*, *30*(5), 26–28.

EPA Chief Information Officer. (2016). EPA National Library Network Policy. CIO Transmittal Number 17-005i, Washington, D.C.: United States Environmental Protection Agency.
Few, S. (2005, November). *Effectively communicating numbers: Selecting the best means of manner and display* [White paper]. Boise, ID: ProClarity.
Halevi, G., Moed, H., & Bar-Ilan, J. (2017). Suitability of Google Scholar as a source of scientific information and as a source of data for scientific evaluation – Review of the Literature. *Journal of Informetrics, 11*(3), 823–834. DOI:10.1016/j.joi.2017.06.005
Headquarters Library. (1994). *EPA library network manual.* Report Number 260-R-95-001. United States Environmental Protection Agency, Washington, DC.
Kostoff, R. (1996). Performance measures for government sponsored research. *Scientometrics, 36*(3), 281–292.
Makar, S., Malinowski, A., & Bhat, T. (2017). Visualization creates an effective impact story. *Information Outlook, 21*(5), 4–7.
Roemer, R., & Borchardt, R. (2015). *Meaningful metrics: A 21st century librarian's guide to bibliometrics, altmetrics, and research impact.* Chicago, IL: Association of College and Research Libraries.
United States Environmental Protection Agency. EPA History. (n.d.). https://www.epa.gov/history
United States Environmental Protection Agency. Milestones in U.S. EPA and Environmental History. (n.d.). https://www.epa.gov/history#timeline
United States Environmental Protection Agency. Resource Conservation and Recovery Act (RCRA) Overview. (n.d.). https://www.epa.gov/rcra/resource-conservation-and-recovery-act-rcra-overview
United States Environmental Protection Agency. The Guardian: Origins of the EPA. (1992). https://archive.epa.gov/epa/aboutepa/guardian-origins-epa.html
United States Environmental Protection Agency. The Origins of EPA. (n.d.). https://www.epa.gov/history/origins-epa

Appendix A

Appendix A1

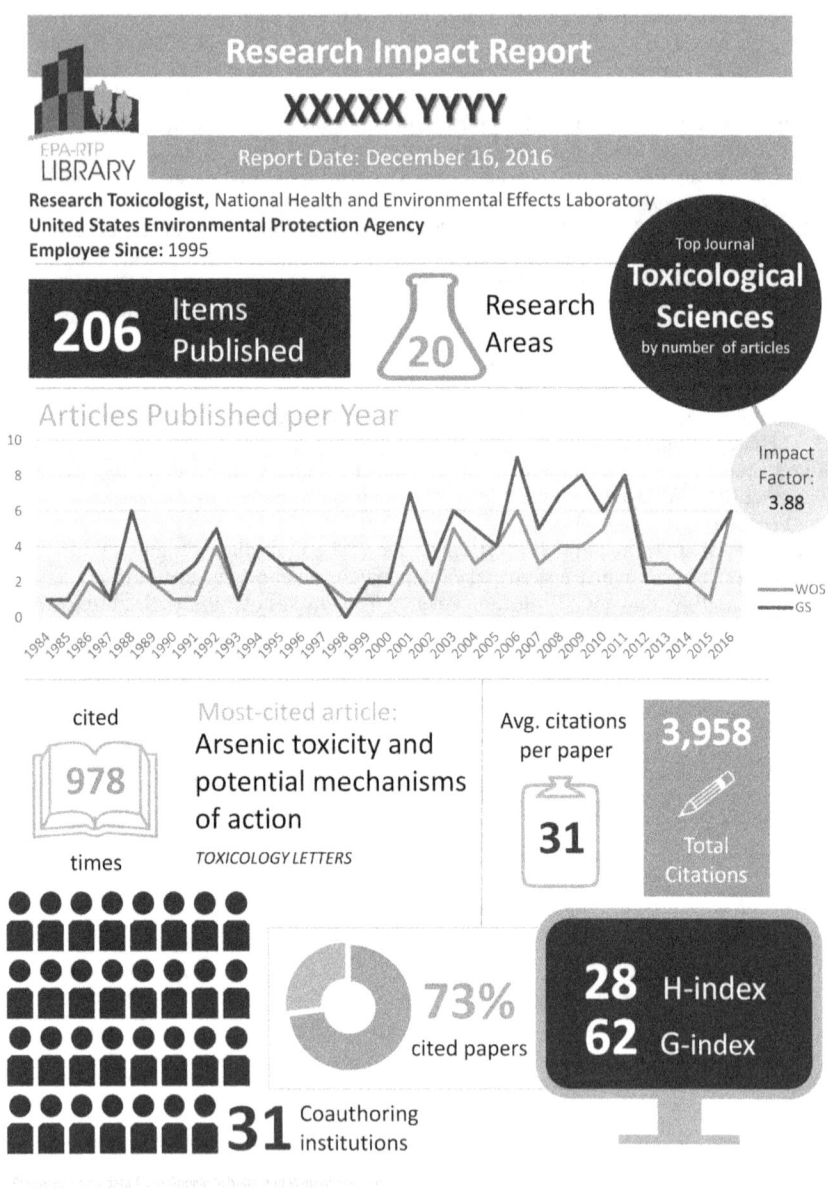

Appendix A2

Research Impact Report – XXXXX YYYY
Prepared by the EPA-RTP Library, December 16, 2016

Overview of Citation Metrics from Web of Science

Results found: 91

Sum of the Times Cited: 2807

Sum of Times Cited without self-citations: 2658

Citing Articles: 2307

Citing Articles without self-citations: 2253

Average Citations per Item: 30.85

H-index: 26

Overview of Citation Metrics from Google Scholar

Results found: 139

Sum of the Times Cited: 3958

Average Citations per Item: 28.47

H-index: 28

G-index: 62

Published Items Each Year from Web of Science

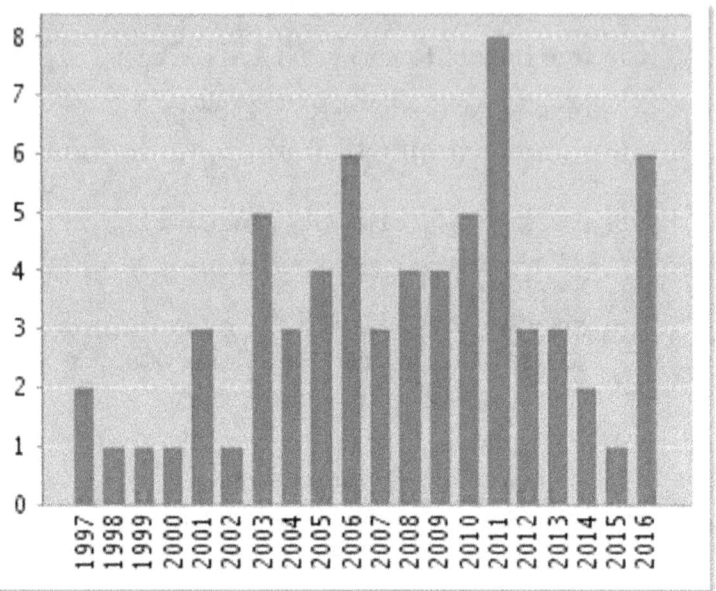

Citations Each Year in Web of Science

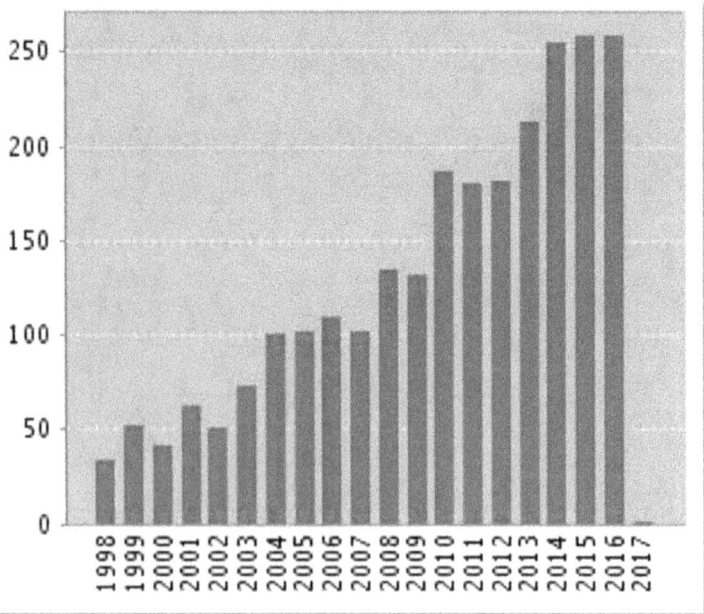

Top Institutional Co-Authors

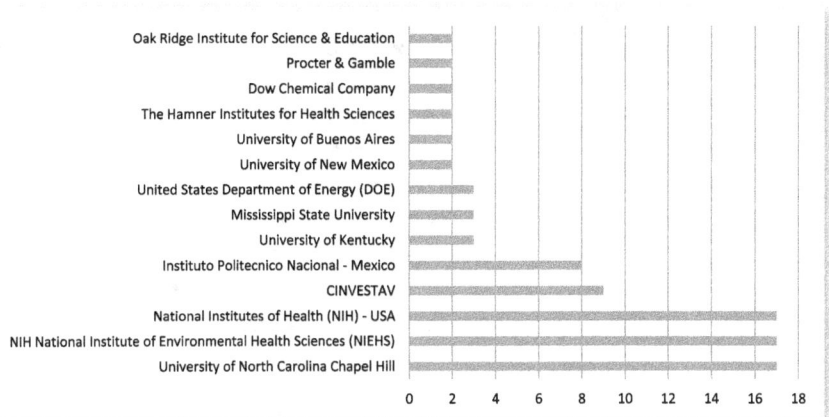

Article Distribution by Research Category

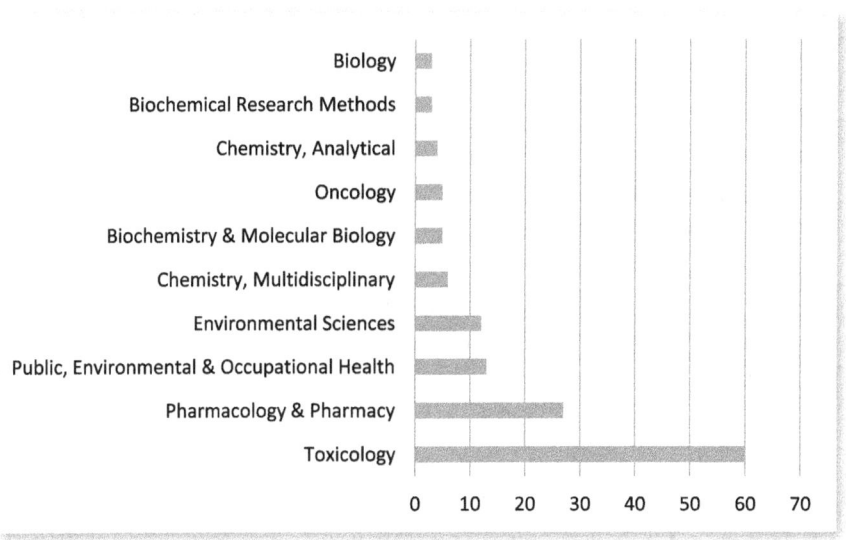

Funding Agency Support by Number of Articles

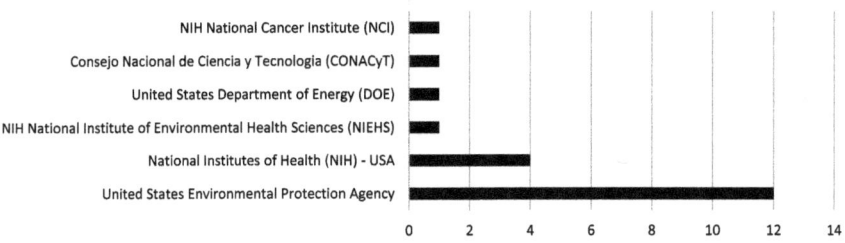

Top Journals by Number of Articles

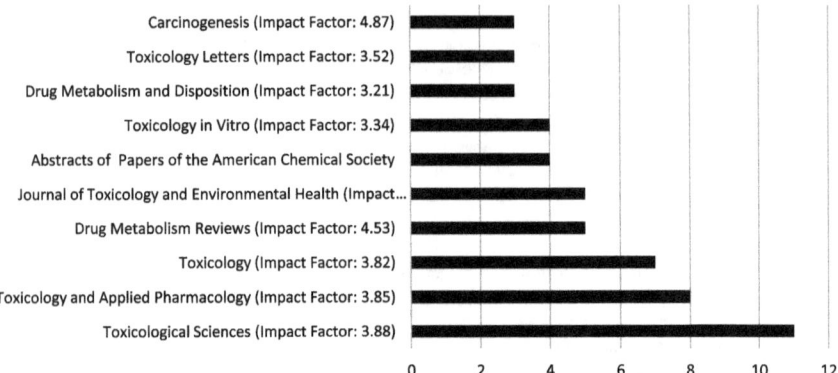

Top Journals by JCR Category Ranking

Journal Title	JCR Category	Journal Rank in Category
Carcinogenesis	Oncology	37
Drug Metabolism and Disposition	Pharmacology & Pharmacy	67
Drug Metabolism Reviews	Pharmacology & Pharmacy	32
Journal of Toxicology and Environmental Health	Environmental Sciences	53
	Public, Environmental & Occupational Health	42
	Toxicology	44
Toxicological Sciences	Toxicology	11
Toxicology	Pharmacology & Pharmacy	51
	Toxicology	13
Toxicology and Applied Pharmacology	Pharmacology & Pharmacy	48
	Toxicology	12
Toxicology in Vitro	Toxicology	19
Toxicology Letters	Toxicology	18
Non-Journals		
Abstracts of Papers of the American Chemical Society		

JCR Metrics for Top Journals

Name	Journal Impact Factor	5 Year Impact Factor	Immediacy Index	Cited Half Life	Article Influence	Eigenfactor
Toxicological Sciences	3.88	4.307	0.903	7.6	1.18	0.02428
Toxicology and Applied Pharmacology	3.847	4.01	0.735	7.9	1.007	0.02387
Toxicology	3.817	3.967	0.912	9	0.999	0.01462
Drug Metabolism Reviews	4.526	5.572	0.559	9.2	1.628	0.0034
Journal of Toxicology and Environmental Health	1.805	2.188	0.275	7.2	0.561	0.00945
Toxicology in Vitro	3.338	3.285	0.715	5.8	0.73	0.01261
Drug Metabolism and Disposition	3.21	3.25	0.966	8.4	0.845	0.01699
Toxicology Letters	3.522	3.571	0.625	7	0.879	0.02027
Carcinogenesis	4.874	5.368	0.967	8	1.517	0.03371

Top 20% Highest Scoring Altmetric Articles

30	Arsenic Exposure and Toxicology: A Historical Perspective **Toxicological Sciences** DOI: 10.1093/toxsci/kfr184	Picked up by **1** news outlet(s) Blogged by **1** Referenced in **1** policy source(s) Tweeted by **12** On **1** Facebook page(s) **270** readers on Mendeley **0** readers on Connotea **0** readers on CiteULike
10	Dose and Effect Thresholds for Early Key Events in a PPARα-Mediated Mode of Action **Toxicological Sciences** DOI: 10.1093/toxsci/kfv236	Picked up by **1** news outlet(s) Tweeted by **1** **3** readers on Mendeley **0** readers on Connotea **0** readers on CiteULike
9	Arsenic toxicity and potential mechanisms of action **Toxicology Letters** DOI: <u>10.1016/s0378-4274(02)00084-x</u>	Referenced in **2** policy source(s) Referenced in **3** Wikipedia pages **267** readers on Mendeley **0** readers on Connotea **0** readers on CiteULike

*Screenshots taken 16 Dec 2016 (current scores and data may vary)

Source name	Definition
Twitter	Collection of tweets, retweets, and quoted tweets with links to scholarly content
Facebook	Monitors Public Facebook Pages and posts
Policy documents	Scans and text-mines policy document PDFs for references; connected to CrossRef and PubMed for DOIs
News	Manually curated data provided from third-parties and RSS feeds
Blogs	Manually curated list, attempts to gather posts linking to scholarly articles
Mendeley	Number of readers with the content in their library
Connotea	Online reference manager counted similar to Mendeley
CiteULike	Online reference manager counted similar to Mendeley
Wikipedia	Mentions located in References section

Top 20% Highly Cited Articles in Web of Science [sample of total output]

Record 1 of 18
Title: Arsenic toxicity and potential mechanisms of action
Author(s): XXXX YYYY
Source: TOXICOLOGY LETTERS **Volume:** 133 **Issue:** 1 **Pages:** 1-16 **Article Number:** PII S0378-4274(02)00084-X **DOI:** 10.1016/S0378-4274(02)00084-X **Published:** JUL 7 2002
Times Cited in Web of Science Core Collection: 563
Total Times Cited: 596
Abstract: Exposure to the metalloid arsenic is a daily occurrence because of its environmental pervasiveness. Arsenic, which is found in several different chemical forms and oxidation states, causes acute and chronic adverse health effects, including cancer. The metabolism of arsenic has an important role in its toxicity. The metabolism involves reduction to a trivalent state and oxidative methylation to a pentavalent state. The trivalent arsenicals, including those methylated, have more potent toxic properties than the pentavalent arsenicals. The exact mechanism of the action of arsenic is not known, but several hypotheses have been proposed. At a biochemical level, inorganic arsenic in the pentavalent state may replace phosphate in several reactions. In the trivalent state, inorganic and organic (methylated) arsenic may react with critical thiols in proteins and inhibit their activity. Regarding cancer, potential mechanisms include genotoxicity, altered DNA methylation, oxidative stress, altered cell proliferation, co-carcinogenesis, and tumor promotion. A better understanding of the mechanism(s) of action of arsenic will make a more confident determination of the risks associated with exposure to this chemical. (C) 2002 Elsevier Science Ireland Ltd. All rights reserved.
Accession Number: WOS:000176959200002
PubMed ID: 12076506
Conference Title: 9th International Congress of Toxicology
Conference Date: JUL 08-12, 2001
Conference Location: BRISBANE, AUSTRALIA
ISSN: 0378-4274

Record 2 of 18
Title: Prostaglandin-H Synthase and Xenobiotic Oxidation
Author(s): XXXX YYYY
Source: ANNUAL REVIEW OF PHARMACOLOGY AND TOXICOLOGY **Volume:** 30 **Pages:** 1-45 **Published:** 1990
Times Cited in Web of Science Core Collection: 264
Total Times Cited: 271
Accession Number: WOS:A1990DA54300001
PubMed ID: 2111654
ISSN: 0362-1642

Record 3 of 18

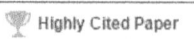

Title: Arsenic Exposure and Toxicology: A Historical Perspective
Author(s): XXXX YYYY
Source: TOXICOLOGICAL SCIENCES **Volume:** 123 **Issue:** 2 **Pages:** 305-332 **DOI:** 10.1093/toxsci/kfr184 **Published:** OCT 2011
Times Cited in Web of Science Core Collection: 221
Total Times Cited: 233

Abstract: The metalloid arsenic is a natural environmental contaminant to which humans are routinely exposed in food, water, air, and soil. Arsenic has a long history of use as a homicidal agent, but in the past 100 years arsenic, has been used as a pesticide, a chemotherapeutic agent and a constituent of consumer products. In some areas of the world, high levels of arsenic are naturally present in drinking water and are a toxicological concern. There are several structural forms and oxidation states of arsenic because it forms alloys with metals and covalent bonds with hydrogen, oxygen, carbon, and other elements. Environmentally relevant forms of arsenic are inorganic and organic existing in the trivalent or pentavalent state. Metabolism of arsenic, catalyzed by arsenic (+3 oxidation state) methyltransferase, is a sequential process of reduction from pentavalency to trivalency followed by oxidative methylation back to pentavalency. Trivalent arsenic is generally more toxicologically potent than pentavalent arsenic. Acute effects of arsenic range from gastrointestinal distress to death. Depending on the dose, chronic arsenic exposure may affect several major organ systems. A major concern of ingested arsenic is cancer, primarily of skin, bladder, and lung. The mode of action of arsenic for its disease endpoints is currently under study. Two key areas are the interaction of trivalent arsenicals with sulfur in proteins and the ability of arsenic to generate oxidative stress. With advances in technology and the recent development of animal models for arsenic carcinogenicity, understanding of the toxicology of arsenic will continue to improve.

Accession Number: WOS:000295532900001
PubMed ID: 21750349
ISSN: 1096-6080
eISSN: 1096-0929

Appendix B

Article Impact Report

Occurrence, genotoxicity, and carcinogenicity of regulated and emerging disinfection by-products in drinking water: A review and roadmap for research

Mutation Research – Reviews in Mutation Research

EPA Author 1, Author 2, Author 3

EPA Author et al. (2007). Occurrence, genotoxicity, and carcinogenicity of regulated and emerging disinfection by-products in drinking water: A review and roadmap for research. Mutation Research/Reviews in Mutation Research, 636(1-3), 178-242. PMID: 17980649 DOI: 10.1016/j.mrrev.2007.09.001

Highlights

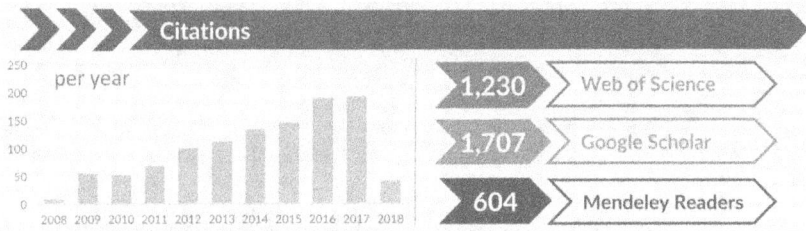

Citations per year (2008–2018)
- 1,230 Web of Science
- 1,707 Google Scholar
- 604 Mendeley Readers

cited in 63 countries by authors from 1,065 organizations across 275 publication titles

18 Altmetric Attention Score

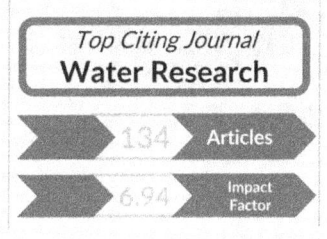

Top Citing Journal
Water Research
134 Articles
6.94 Impact Factor

7 citations in international patents

Citations by Country

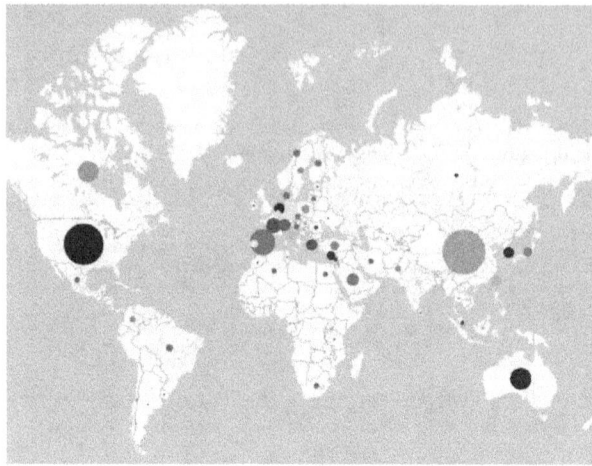

Countries	Papers
CHINA	355
USA	309
SPAIN	123
AUSTRALIA	86
CANADA	85
ENGLAND	65
GERMANY	63
FRANCE	43
ITALY	41
SAUDI ARABIA	29

Top Citing Organizations

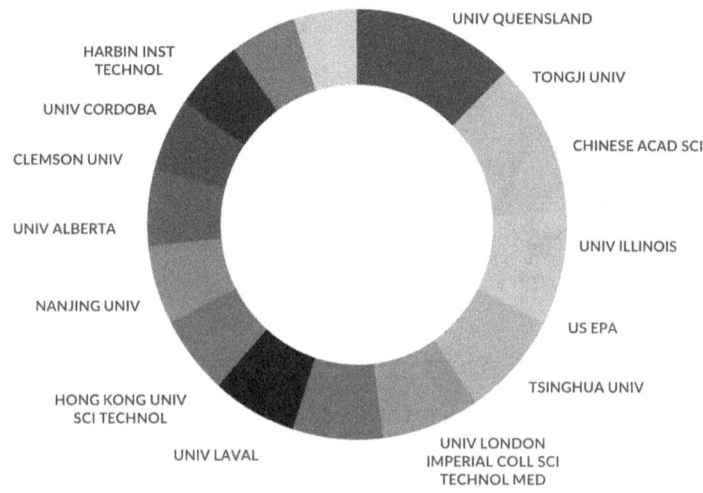

A Breath of Fresh Air

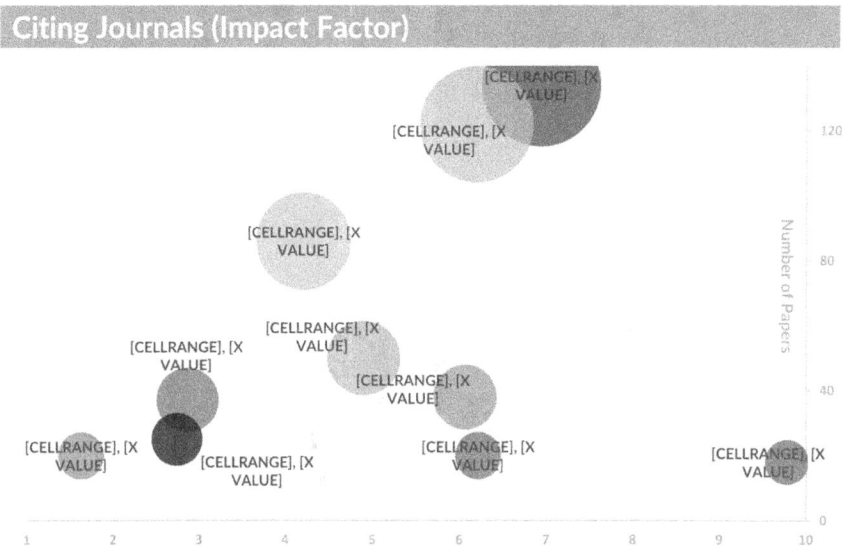

Citing Journals (Impact Factor)

Research Areas

Research Areas	Papers
ENVIRON SCIENCES ECOLOGY	735
ENGINEERING	472
WATER RESOURCES	286
CHEMISTRY	146
TOXICOLOGY	106
PUBLIC, ENVIRON, OCCUP HEALTH	85
BIOCHEM MOL BIOLOGY	40
SCIENCE, TECHN OTHER TOPICS	31
BIOTECHNOL APPLIED MICROBIOL	24
GENETICS HEREDITY	21

Alternative Metrics

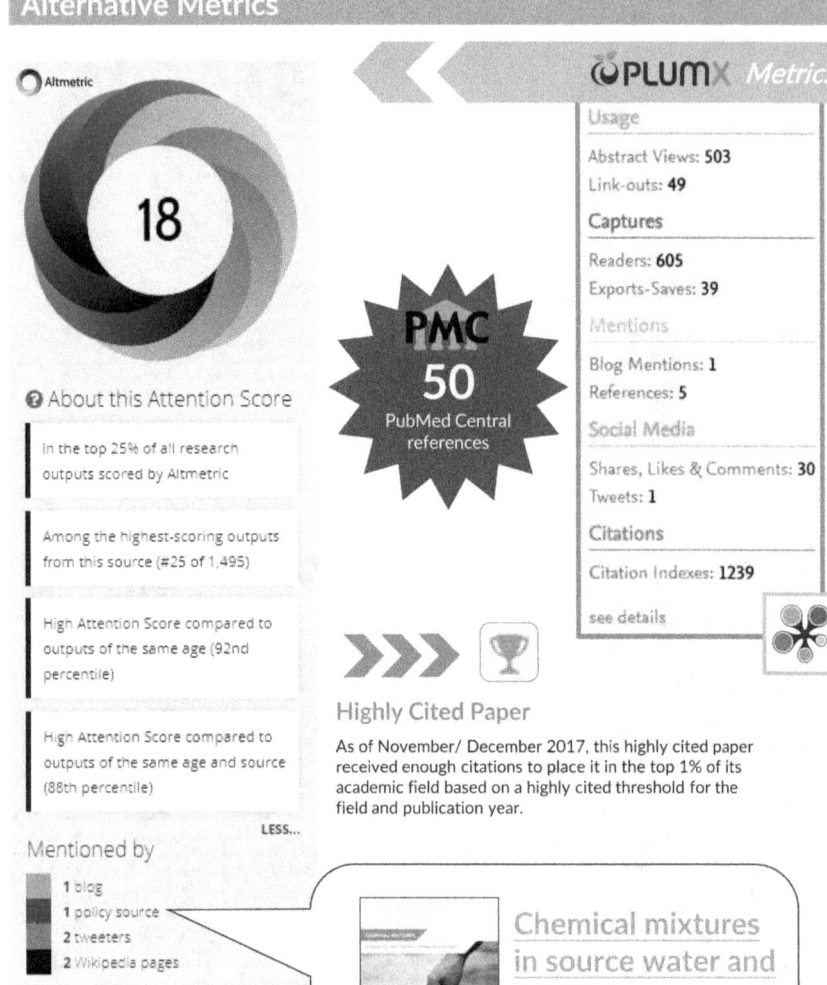

About the Report

This report was compiled using data from Web of Science, Google Scholar, Altmetric, and other databases when necessary. It is a snapshot of a particular article where the impact has been determined through analyzing various information about the papers citing that article. By collecting and organizing these statistics, a picture of reach, popularity, and value is created.

Citations by Country

The origin of the citing papers as determined by author addresses. All records are shown on the graphic, and the logical threshold is displayed in the accompanying table.

Top Citing Organizations

The listed author affiliations of citing articles. Percentage is determined using a logical threshold where the remaining percent of the whole would be considered "other."

Citing Journals

The volume of citing papers per the top ten journal titles compared to other titles citing the paper, displayed along with the journal's impact factor for the report year. In the graphic:
- position along the x axis is determined by the journal impact factor
- position along the y axis is determined by the number of citing papers published in the source title
- size is determined by the percentage of citing papers published in the specific source title compared to all other titles

Research Areas

The scientific category for each citing paper. A logical threshold is displayed in the graphic, and an expansion is shown in the accompanying table.

Alternative Metrics

Metrics gathered using the Altmetric database, PlumX Analytics, publisher website data, and other sources including but not limited to those listed in the Altmetric doughnut:

Source name	Definition
Twitter	Collection of tweets, retweets, and quoted tweets with links to scholarly content
Facebook	Monitors Public Facebook Pages and posts
Policy documents	Scans and text-mines policy document PDFs for references; connected to CrossRef and PubMed for DOIs
News	Manually curated data provided from third-parties and RSS feeds
Blogs	Manually curated list, attempts to gather posts linking to scholarly articles
Mendeley	Number of readers with the content in their library
Connotea	Discontinued online reference manager
CiteULike	Online reference manager counted similar to Mendeley
Wikipedia	Mentions located in References section
Google+	Mentions from public posts

Appendix C

Article Impact Report

Fluorinated Compounds in U.S. Fast Food Packaging
Environmental Science & Technology Letters

EPA Author 1, EPA Author 2, EPA Author 3

EPA Author et al. (2017). Fluorinated Compounds in U.S. Fast Food Packaging. *Environmental Science & Technology Letters* 4(3), 105-111. PMID: 30148183 DOI: 10.1021/acs.estlett.6b00435

Highlights

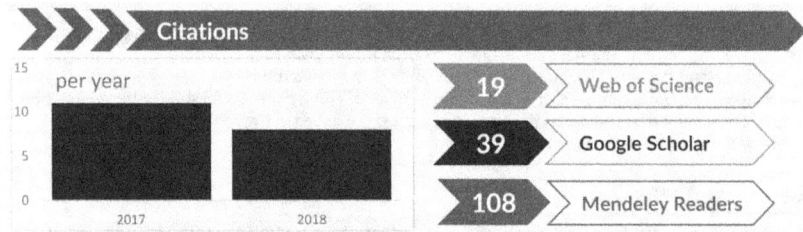

cited in 17 countries — by authors from **47 organizations** across **14 publication titles**

986 Altmetric Attention Score

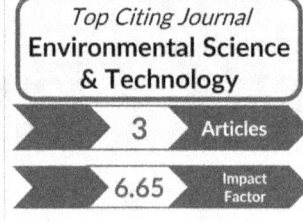

Top Citing Journal
Environmental Science & Technology
3 Articles
6.65 Impact Factor

Picked up in 99 news articles

Alternative Metrics

986

🛈 About this Attention Score

In the top 5% of all research outputs scored by Altmetric

One of the highest-scoring outputs from this source (#3 of 314)

High Attention Score compared to outputs of the same age (99th percentile)

High Attention Score compared to outputs of the same age and source (91st percentile)

LESS...

Mentioned by
- 99 news outlets
- 9 blogs
- 1 policy source
- 187 tweeters
- 37 Facebook pages
- 3 Google+ users
- 1 Redditor

Citations
- 27 Dimensions

Readers on
- 108 Mendeley
- 1 CiteULike

Screenshot taken 24 Oct 2018
(current score and data may vary)

TIME Magazine — Here's Another Reason to Avoid Fast Food
February 2, 2017

Forbes — How Fast Food Wrapping And Packaging Can Be Bad For Your Health
February 2, 2017

CNN News — Chemicals found in one-third of fast food packaging, report finds
February 1, 2017

Highly Cited Paper

As of May/June 2018, this highly cited paper received enough citations to place it in the top 1% of the academic field of **Environment/Ecology** based on a highly cited threshold for the field and publication year in Web of Science.

Toxicological profile for perfluoroalkyls: draft for public comment
Centers for Disease Control and Prevention
June 2018

Appendix D

EPA Document Impact Report

Integrated Science Assessment for Ozone and Related Photochemical Oxidants
Environmental Protection Agency

National Center for Environmental Assessment—RTP Division

U.S. EPA. Integrated Science Assessment (ISA) of Ozone and Related Photochemical Oxidants (Final Report, Feb 2013). U.S. Environmental Protection Agency, Washington, DC, EPA/600/R-10/076F, 2013.

Highlights

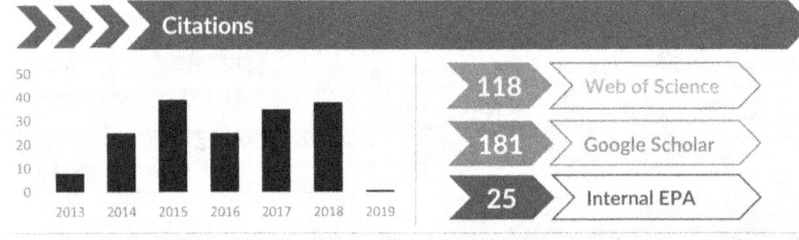

Citations
- 118 Web of Science
- 181 Google Scholar
- 25 Internal EPA

by authors from **512 organizations** across **89 publication titles**

including **11 articles** from

Atmospheric Environment
3.70 Impact Factor

Top Research Areas

Environmental Science
Meteorology/Atmospheric Science
Public Environmental & Occupational Health Science
Toxicology
Environmental Engineering

by number of articles 0 10 20 30 40 50 60 70

Chapter 5

Compliance and Defiance: Michigan Publishing's Early Encounters with Research Impact Metrics

Rebecca Welzenbach and Charles Watkinson

Introduction

This chapter describes how Michigan Publishing, the primary scholarly publishing unit at the University of Michigan (U-M), has engaged with scholarly metrics to understand and communicate the impact of our monographs, journals, and other publications. Michigan Publishing is a division of the U-M Library and consists of the U-M Press, Michigan Publishing Services, and our institutional repository, called Deep Blue. As a scholarly publisher at the intersection of tradition and innovation, our main strengths and interests lie in two major areas:

- Publishing and supporting excellent and innovative scholarship in the humanities and social sciences, including:
  - Developing and publishing peer-reviewed scholarly *monographs* in the humanities and social sciences, with particular disciplinary strengths.
  - Producing and hosting independent, open-access (OA) *journals* in the humanities and social sciences, with particular strengths in philosophy, Asian studies, and media studies.
  - Sustaining access to a durable, digital scholarly record of the scholarly output of the U-M available in perpetuity to the broadest possible audience, via our *institutional repository, Deep Blue*.

- Driving change in our industry to help university presses and library publishers adapt and thrive into the future, including:
  - Exploring and promoting *new business models* for sustainable scholarly publishing through the development of *community-owned scholarly infrastructure* that meets the changing needs of authors and readers and aligns with their values.

○ *Modeling leadership and collaboration* in both the university press and library publishing communities through joint research projects and initiatives with peer organizations (About – Michigan Publishing, 2017).

In this chapter, we provide history and context for the experience, assumptions, and expectations that Michigan Publishing brings to the scholarly metrics conversation. As well, we describe some early experiments and what we have learned from them, and look ahead to our future plans as changing internal and external factors compel us to capture and report more and more data about the impact of our publications and services.

Here is the short version: in their current form, citation-based measures of research impact do not yet adequately represent or serve Michigan Publishing's books, journals, programs, or stakeholders. There is just not enough consistent, reliable data, and humanities-oriented monograph publishers as a community have not yet established the norms to interpret what data exists and communicate it effectively. However, as new platforms and tools emerge, what we can know about our publications is changing rapidly. In addition, entirely new ways of measuring impact and success allow us to engage with research impact metrics in ways that better represent our work and values.

At Michigan Publishing, we care deeply about understanding the impact of our publications and communicating that information to authors, peers, funders, and institutional leadership. And, with our peer publishers, we are actively wrestling with how best to accomplish this. We are eager to explore new measures of impact, from usage statistics and download counts for online publications to altmetrics and, especially, indicators of reach beyond our local campus and the academy, such as influence on policy documents. Demand for research impact metrics is only increasing, driven by government mandates such as the UK's Research Excellence Framework, by funding agencies, and by authors and researchers who themselves are facing new requirements to provide evidence of the impact of their work.

We see two paths for us to meet this demand more effectively: First, we can work to ensure that our publications are consistently recognized by and included in the systems and datasets upon which existing metrics are calculated. As we will discuss below, this is not always reasonable or even possible – but it is an avenue that must be considered. Second, we can articulate new (alternative) metrics that are meaningful for us and our stakeholders, and which we *are* able to consistently capture and report. This path allows us to focus on the data points that are meaningful to us, and to develop an appropriate metrics strategy from the start, rather than reproducing weaknesses of existing metrics, or shoehorning our publications into systems that may not represent them well. It is also an opportunity for us to exemplify and advocate for responsible, nuanced, and contextualized reporting on the impact of our work.

What is Michigan Publishing?

Michigan Publishing is the scholarly publishing division of the U-M Library. It consists of the U-M Press, Michigan Publishing Services, and our institutional repository, called Deep Blue. Michigan Publishing is led by the Associate University Librarian for Publishing and Director of the U-M Press, who reports to the Dean of Libraries. This combined organization was formed in 2009, when the university press began reporting to the Dean of Libraries and, after several years of evolution, emerged as a fully integrated library division in 2013. However, each of Michigan Publishing's constituent parts has a longstanding history of its own.

The U-M Press, established in 1930, has long been known for its strengths in the areas of performing arts, media studies, political science, classical studies, American studies (including sub-fields such as disability studies), and area studies (especially Asian, African, and German studies). The press also has a world-class line of English Language Teaching books and course materials and a vibrant trade publishing list focused on the Great Lakes region of the Midwest US, though these product lines are quite distinct from our scholarly monographs and therefore are not addressed in this chapter. U-M Press monographs are published in hardcover, softcover, and ebook formats. As of January 2019, the press is one of just a few university presses to offer its own independently hosted comprehensive ebook collection (McKenzie, 2018). While most U-M Press titles are offered via a traditional sales model, the press also publishes an increasing number of OA monographs, dating back to 2006 with the launch of the OA digitalculturebooks series. Today, the press publishes about 100 new titles per year, of which a growing portion are published on an OA basis through the sponsorship of a variety of programs, including Knowledge Unlatched, the Humanities Open Book Program sponsored by the National Endowment for the Humanities and the Andrew W. Mellon Foundation, and the Toward an Open Monograph Ecosystem (TOME) initiative, through which 15 universities have committed up to three grants of $15,000.00 per year to offset the costs of publishing OA monographs (Participating Colleges and Universities, 2018).

The press consists of several units: Acquisitions, Production, and Marketing & Outreach. Within the Acquisitions unit, a group of acquiring editors and editorial associates work together to build relationships with authors, contract new titles, manage the peer review and revision process, and ultimately get the manuscript in the door and approved by the press's editorial board. Production, including a managing editor, production editors, designers, and a production associate, handles all the work to transform the manuscript into its final print and electronic formats. Marketing & Outreach is responsible for delivering the book to its audience, from handling individual promotions, reviews, and submissions for awards, to visibility and author events at conferences, to the press catalog and website. Additionally, the press (along with all of Michigan Publishing) is supported by a Business & Administration office and a technology group, who develop, support, and manage the software applications (both homegrown and licensed) that support our business.

Michigan Publishing Services (MPS) is the descendant of the U-M Library's Scholarly Publishing Office (SPO), which was formed in 2001 to support experiments in online, OA publishing. SPO collaborated with forward-thinking scholars to launch such projects as *Philosophers' Imprint*, the first open access journal in its field; the *Encyclopedia of Diderot and D'Alembert Collaborative Translation Project*, an OA, crowd-sourced digital humanities translation project; and the *Influenza Encyclopedia*, a digital history project (Publications, 2017). Today, MPS provides hosting and publishing services to more than 30 online, OA serials, and has worked with partners across the U-M campus to publish 34 books, conference proceedings, and other projects. MPS also provides production and hosting support to external clients including Lever Press and Humanities EBook. MPS staff have a variety of experience in electronic publishing and workflow management and the director is a librarian.

The *Deep Blue* institutional repository was launched in 2006, with the aim of creating a comprehensive record of scholarship published by U-M affiliates, preserved and, where possible, made open to the public, by the library. At the end of 2018, Deep Blue contained more than 121,000 objects, from across all disciplines. Among institutional repositories, Deep Blue was a pioneer in negotiating directly with publishers to acquire "back" journal articles authored by U-M affiliates, along with the right to make them available in the repository. In addition to these research articles published in major journals, about one-third of the items in Deep Blue have not been published anywhere else. These items often take the form of research outputs other than journal articles, such as conference papers, datasets, white papers, and research reports, such as those from the U-M Transportation Research Institute. The Deep Blue repository is split between two software systems; one focused on documents and the other on data sets. The document repository is built on the DSpace framework while the data repository is constructed in the Samvera Fedora framework. Known since late 2018 as Deep Blue Repository and Research Data Services, the initiative is staffed by several librarians and one full-time repositories assistant, with support from a developer in our Library Information Technology unit who manages the back end of the systems.

As we consider how metrics of impact are incorporated into Michigan Publishing's work and strategy, it is important to understand the variety of professional backgrounds, training, and experiences that make up this unique organization. This heterogeneity is core to the Michigan Publishing identity, and informs the ways we think about and seek to measure success. For the remainder of this chapter, then, we will address how each aspect of Michigan Publishing is implicated in capturing and communicating the impact of our publications both in ways that align with the established paradigm of research impact metrics ("compliance") and that rely on new or alternative data points ("defiance") that we anticipate will better serve our needs and those of our stakeholders, now and in the future.

Monographs

Compliance

For those more accustomed to the journal publishing sphere, it may come as a real shock to realize how far removed scholarly monographs and university presses are from the culture of citation-based measures of impact. In order to understand where university presses currently stand with respect to impact metrics, it is vital to recognize – and it is probably difficult to overstate – this separation. Most major citation indexes were designed for journal articles and, as a result, historically there has simply been little (or no) data for us to gather from these indexes, and therefore little reason to engage with these systems. Today, many of these tools have started to find ways to include books, either as part of their main product: Scopus started indexing books in 2013 (Elsevier Announces its Scopus Book Expansion Program, 2013); or as an alternative product, such as Clarivate's Book Citation Index – Humanities and Social Sciences (BKCI-SSH), launched in 2011. BKCI-SSH tracks monographs, integrating with Web of Science (WoS) Core Collection data to track citations. However, this is a selective resource and focuses only the years 2005 and forward. As a result, the vast majority of our press' titles are omitted. As of 2018, only 194 U-M Press titles appear in the BKCI-SSH – on the order of 5% of our total catalog. Additionally, only citations in articles from the WoS Core Collection and from BKCI-SSH itself are counted. Citations that occur in other books or journal articles outside of these sources are not tracked. Because of the very limited representation of both our own books and the other publications most likely to cite them, the metrics available in BKCI-SSH have not yet provided meaningful data to our press or our authors. In contrast, Scopus has indexed 916 U-M Press titles dating back to 1983, along with citation counts for each. As of 2016, all U-M Press book metadata is submitted to Scopus for indexing as a matter of course.

In the last five years, two new platforms have changed the conversation and the culture around citation-based impact measures for books. The first is Google Scholar, which (by way of Google Books) has since 2013 indexed metadata about essentially all U-M Press books. Google Scholar also attempts to identify citations for all the books it has indexed. More recently, in January 2018, the launch of DimensionsPlus from Digital Science brought together various research-related data sources (over 138 million pieces thus far) in a venue that is consistent and accessible to the community. In addition to deep-indexing, the Dimensions team invests in enhancing existing data for increased searchability and identifying links between related pieces (nearly 4 billion connections so far) (Dimensions, 2018).

DimensionsPlus explicitly seeks to capture information beyond the typical scholarly publication and citation landscape, including policy documents, patents, grants, clinical trials, Altmetric data, and more. Through an agreement with ReadCube, Digital Science's reading platform, the U-M Press has made most of its books visible to Dimensions for indexing. Likewise, the press has decided to display Dimensions badges on its website's book details pages where applicable. This means that as of spring 2018, for the first time, anyone can see the Dimensions citation count for our monographs on our own website:

Fig. 1: According to Dimensions, the 2003 book *Cops, Teachers, Counselors: Stories from the Front Lines of Public Service* has been cited 327 times by other publications also indexed by Dimensions.

Including U-M Press books in emerging tools like DimensionsPlus makes it possible for us to explore citation-based metrics that previously we simply did not have the data to consider. But it also means we now have to wrestle with these data and how it is represented in ways we never did before. A few years ago, no one would have expected to find a citation count on a university press's book web page. It is certainly not the kind of information that our authors would typically expect to see so publicly posted. In many ways this is an exciting development, but we are already beginning to observe that authors (and their home institutions), readers, and others have questions about what these numbers mean, and how they should be used. In order to build goodwill with our authors and persuade them of the value of displaying these data, we need to feel confident that the numbers are accurate and expressed clearly.

Unfortunately, in a space where the book itself and the network in which it is likely to be cited are only partially represented, and where there is no agreed upon authoritative source, the citation information can vary wildly. For example, let us look at how **BKCI-SSH**, **Scopus**, **Google Scholar**, and **DimensionsPlus** each capture citation information about a U-M Press title from 2013, *Partisan Gerrymandering and the Construction of American Democracy*, by Erik J. Engstrom. In this case, BKCI-SSH captures 12 citations, all in journals indexed in the WoS Core Collection. Scopus counts only eight citations, five of which are journal articles and three of which are books. Google Scholar finds 22 citations in journals, books, an article in an institutional repository, and an article posted on a faculty website. DimensionsPlus (the source we display on our website) identifies seven citations. Of these, five overlap with the citations found in BKCI-SSH (the other two are book reviews) and four overlap with the citations in Scopus. Of course, journal articles are subject to the very same sort of variance: different sets of citation data will naturally return different total citation counts. But precisely because monographs are so marginalized in this space, it seems much more likely that important nodes in the citation network – notably, other monographs – might well be missed. As well, because there is no accepted authoritative source for monograph bibliographic and citation data, and because bibliometric analysis is newer and less trusted in the humanities monograph space than in the journal world, these discrepancies understandably cause a lot of consternation within our organization and for our authors. In short, there is a lot of exciting opportunity here, and the landscape is changing rapidly, but we do not yet have any system of citation-based metrics that adequately reflects the reach and impact of our monographs. Moreover, as a publisher, while of course we want to know that our books have made their way into the scholarly literature, there are often data points other than citations that have captured our attention.

Defiance

As a publisher, what we are interested in measuring, and the story we want to tell about our publications, is a bit different from what an individual author or researcher wants to report about their own work. While we do want to know about the success of individual titles, for us it is also imperative to report on our effectiveness as an organization, a business, and a suite of programs and services. Historically, the measures used by university presses to indicate success reflect on individual titles to a certain extent, but are best taken together to report on the success of the organization as a whole.

U-M Press and its peers have typically measured the impact and success of monographs in the following ways:

- *Financial,* across Michigan Publishing. Do we sell enough books to survive? To answer this question, it is important to look across the whole, rather than at each title individually. For scholarly publishers, financial success must always be interpreted in the aggregate; the success or failure of individual books does not reveal much about the overall health of the publisher, since it is typical that a few highly successful books will offset losses from other books that may be important, but less marketable.

- *Academic and disciplinary reputation/prestige.* How do our books fare compared to other books in the same discipline? This is best understood by way of indicators such as reviews in prominent outlets, awards, course adoptions, winning author contracts against competitor presses, and repeat/return authors.
- *Usage, adoption, and persistence.* What can we say about who is using our books, and how? Do books remain popular over time? Is there good reason to issue them in new formats, as new editions, or in translation?

For most of the history of the press, there was very little that we could know about this last bullet point beyond counting the sales of the book itself. But now that we offer electronic versions of essentially our entire catalog, we can learn a great deal from web analytics about who is using our books, how they discover them, and more. In the last four years or so, we have also become especially interested in taking advantage of our arrangements with ebook vendor platforms to learn more about the usage of our books. Although we are interested in these data for all of our books, we have tended to focus on the subset of OA books because it is a manageable list; there is more to explore with books that are available openly on the web; and (most importantly) because OA books are the ones for which it is imperative that we learn how to obtain meaningful usage data because we know that sales of those titles only reveal a small portion of the picture of engagement and use. Rather than insufficient data, our most recent challenge has been figuring out how to make sense of far too much information. We can accumulate the data, but cleaning it, interpreting it, asking the right questions, and using our findings to inform our next steps is a huge undertaking.

In 2016–2017, we partnered with Unglue.it and Open Book Publishers on a one-year research project called Mapping the Free Ebook Supply Chain, supported financially by the Andrew W. Mellon Foundation (Mapping the Free Ebook Supply Chain, 2017). Driven by our observation that OA ebooks drop out of the usual publishing supply chain because that system has not been able to include books that are free, in this project we sought to gather and explore all the quantitative and qualitative information that we could gather about who was using our open access books and how. According to the final project report, a particular focus was on learning whether free ebooks are succeeding in extending the reach of scholarly literature to users who might not otherwise encounter or be able to access it. Using a sample of books published by Open Book Publishers (OBP) and University of Michigan Press (UMP) (including some Open Humanities Press books), the researchers applied a range of quantitative and qualitative techniques: we compiled multiple sources of sales and usage data and conducted analyses on the dataset to try and find patterns; designed and deployed an open source survey tool to solicit responses from ebook users; conducted interviews with a sample of ebook users who had identified themselves through the surveys or on social media; and interviewed a range of vendors to understand how traditional supply chain partners are engaging (or not) with open access books (Watkinson, Welzenbach, Hellman, & Gatti, 2017, p. 1.)

Overall, our findings indicated that usage of the books was "spiky," with most titles exhibiting "extreme non-normal distributions." In other words, as publishers have long suspected, every book is different, and it is not appropriate to make statistical claims about usage across the whole (Watkinson et al., 2017, pp. 1–2). This was one of our first dedicated efforts to collaborate with others on the challenge of gathering and analyzing usage data, and perhaps the most important finding of all was simply how difficult it was to do. The variation in publisher, vendor, and platform behavior around standards and policies for gathering and sharing data was striking, even with just two publishers and a small handful of distribution platforms. The most important outcome of this project then was a case to be made for monograph publishers to work together to establish norms and shared practices for making sense of the usage data that we expect will be so important to our stories of impact going forward.

In addition to exploring new approaches for capturing, interpreting, and communicating usage data for our ebooks, in 2016, we first launched a pilot of Altmetric for Publishers (Ruff, 2016). The pilot consisted of tracking each of our monograph titles (by way of the details page on the press website), and displaying the Altmetric badge there, where there was an Altmetric Attention Score to display. We also made use of the Altmetric Explorer for Publishers dashboard to generate reports on the publications receiving the most attention on the web each week. Because we had a limited number of seats to access this dashboard, one staff member would create and circulate the report each week. Our key takeaways from this experiment were to identify where engagement on the web – especially in the news and in policy documents – can help us report on the effectiveness and global reach of OA books. The tool can also help us make decisions about new editions or updated versions of books, especially when we observe sustained or renewed interest in and use of older books by way of inclusion on syllabi, which Altmetric tracks via the Open Syllabus Project. In 2018, our Altmetric Explorer for Publishers pilot was rolled into a campus-wide pilot of Altmetric Explorer for Institutions. This expansion significantly broadened access to the Explorer dashboard, allowing more people to directly engage with Altmetric data and reports and lowering the barrier to access for staff who are just learning how to navigate this space.

Over the last few years, the U-M Press has explored many different avenues for obtaining, gathering, and understanding data about the impact of our monographs, and tried to use that data to answer a variety of questions, from the financial health of our business, to the longevity of an individual work of scholarship, to the discoverability of open versus closed ebooks. These data are obtained from a wide variety of sources, in as many shapes, forms, and formats, and our biggest challenge at this stage is in imagining how to aggregate these data appropriately and present them in meaningful ways to the right audiences. Over the last four years we have made important steps forward in the data we are able to collect, but have yet to arrive at a satisfactory solution for how to analyze it, use it to inform decision making, and present it to various stakeholders. We see major benefits to tackling this work in a coordinated way that employs transparent methods and open standards. In the coming years we anticipate a focus on collaboration with our peer publishers to develop shared mechanisms to gather, analyze, and share these data, to all of our benefits.

Journals

Compliance

Unlike monographs, journals do, of course, have a well-established history and set of standards around bibliometric analysis and research impact metrics. However, again, because of our historical focus on scholarship in the humanities, as well as our long practice of operating as a very lean, web-based journal publisher using a homegrown platform, we do not have a great deal of experience engaging with typical journal bibliometrics. And, for the most part, our editors and authors have not minded this much. However, our occasional journal collaborations in new fields have pushed us to develop new knowledge and functionality in this arena.

For example, in 2015–2016 we launched the *Michigan Journal of Medicine*, an OA, online journal edited by, and focused on publishing the research of, U-M medical students. As researchers, students, and faculty at one of the nation's top medical schools, the founding editorial board and faculty advisors naturally assumed that their brand new student-edited journal would be indexed in Scopus, WoS, and PubMed and would have a competitive Journal Impact Factor (JIF). It had not occurred to them that any legitimate scholarly journal would *not* have these things. We have had a similar experience with a clinical psychology journal that was dropped by a commercial publisher, converted to OA, and joined our portfolio in 2012. Since then – literally, since then – we have been trying to get the journal re-listed in Scopus, re-activated in PsycInfo, and re-indexed in WoS, so that they can get a JIF (they have been accepted for the Emerging Sources Citation Index and in the near future will be re-evaluated for inclusion in the WoS Collection). The next step is to get the journal included in Medline – yet another challenge.

Our journal editors look to us for expertise about indexing, but our experience thus far has been that the application process requires a huge investment of time and energy, rejection is common, and the process takes months or years. It is by no means straightforward or, to our editors' surprise, guaranteed that even a rigorously edited journal will be selected for inclusion. For new journals, especially in the health sciences and adjacent fields, this can become a self-defeating cycle: omission from these indexes becomes a real obstacle to soliciting submissions, since authors are likely to want to publish only in journals with a JIF. And yet, regular, timely publication is the first and most important criterion for inclusion in Web of Science – a difficult bar to meet for those struggling to drum up submissions. For some journals, it is clearly worth the effort. For others, it may not be.

In these cases, we have sometimes found it challenging to talk with our publishing partners about why it takes time and is often difficult to gain acceptance to the desired indexes. Moreover, because inclusion in Scopus and WoS is often the only framework for authority and credibility that these researchers have, it can be a challenge for us as a publisher to demonstrate authority and credibility with new publishing partners when our publications are excluded. This is generally not an issue in the humanities disciplines, but it is a major obstacle to working with journals in STEM fields. We now make it part of our early consultations with potential publishing partners to discuss their expectations (and the standards in their fields) for indexing. When we better understand their needs, assumptions, and expectations, we can better manage their expectations for what is involved and what they will need to do. We cannot always promise that the journal will appear in the desired index, but we can commit to working together toward that goal, looking together at the selection criteria and application process as a guiding plan for our work on the journal.

Our handful of publishing partners in STEM fields, and especially those in the health sciences, are the ones pushing us most proactively toward indexing with WoS, Scopus, and PubMed. But they are not the only ones approaching us to ask about impact factors and other bibliometrics. The others who ask, though, tend to lead us to a very different conversation. Typically what happens is a journal editor who has never before shown any interest in these indices suddenly hears something, or has a requirement imposed upon them, or is comparing themselves against some external party. They turn to us for help and information because they may not understand exactly what this new benchmark is, and how it applies to them. Often, they are hoping we can provide them with a quick and straightforward solution. They are very likely to frame their question as "What is our Impact Factor?" as opposed to "How do we get an Impact Factor?" Their assumption is frequently that they already have a JIF – even if they have never needed this before and do not really understand what it is. In these cases, we can provide guidance and education about how these numbers are calculated, how to pursue indexing, and where to find selection criteria and guidelines, etc. But these conversations tend to be unsatisfactory for these editors, who may not see the long-term value in working toward these criteria – they are looking for a number, usually instantly, in order to persuade an author to agree to go forward with publication. We have a responsibility to continue to improve our education/outreach, as well as our publishing practices and infrastructure, to help our journals meet the selection criteria for indices like WoS and Scopus more easily – but at the same time, as the long-time publisher of journals that do not fit well into the commercial journal publishing world, we have seen firsthand the ways that these bibliometrics do not do much to help our journal editors accomplish what they want to do.

Defiance

Michigan Publishing Services has long been, by its very nature, an experiment in an experimental field: library publishing. As such, we have always been seeking to demonstrate its value to the library, to our campus, and to our partners. Over the years, our indicators for the overall success of our journals program have typically focused on answering the following questions:

- How many publications (typically OA journals) are we publishing? How much has our portfolio grown? It is worth noting that even a simple count of publications is not a terribly revealing metric because some journals publish more than others by nearly an order of magnitude, and likewise some are much more complex to produce than others. So while the number of titles in our portfolio is a useful baseline number for reporting, it actually reveals very little about where and how we spend our effort and expertise.
- What is the turnover? How many new publications launch each year, and how many fold or leave for another publisher? Is there net balance, growth, or shrinkage?
- How many supported publications are written or edited on our campus as opposed to based elsewhere? (In other words, to what extent do our services directly support researchers on our campus, versus elsewhere?)
- How do these publications perform in terms of traditional bibliometrics? When we ask this question of ourselves, we are less interested in assessing how high quality or impactful the scholarship within a journal is, but rather in how successful we as a program have been at getting the publications into the right channels. In other words, in this case these metrics are not really a proxy for scholarly impact, but rather for "to what extent do the editor and publisher have their act together?"

Around 2010, in response to many requests from editors as well as our own curiosity, we started experimenting with Google Analytics. This was our first attempt to provide information about journal usage back to our publishing partners. We could tell them where in the world readers were coming from, the number of views in a given time period, most-read articles ranked in order, and more. In most cases, we heard that this information was particularly useful to editors reporting to boards, funding agencies, administrators, applying for tenure, etc. These metrics were not necessarily of great interest or use to the individual authors of articles themselves – not least because it was quite difficult to share the information with them. Reporting to editors at the journal level was often the best we could do, and even then the reports were often unattractive and difficult to read. This situation improved dramatically with the arrival of Google Data Studio in 2017. For the first time, we could create dynamic, automatically updated, visually appealing reports, visible to anyone (editors, authors, readers, institutions, etc.) at a publicly accessible link. This quarterly report for the *Journal of Electronic Publishing* was set up in the winter of 2017, but continues to update dynamically to reflect the most recent quarter of usage. The online report can be seen at *https://datastudio.google.com/u/ 0/reporting/0B2-RN0tdanSiUFdXVGhPTTNuSmM/page/1ckC*

Incorporating Google Analytics transformed the way we were able to talk about usage of our journals. But this work never felt clear, easy, or user friendly for our stakeholders until Google Data Studio allowed the introduction of these custom reports. This exemplifies a situation we have found ourselves in frequently: there is a lot of data being tracked every minute and, with the help of powerful tools like Google Analytics, it can be relatively easy to accrue masses of it. But none of that is terribly helpful to us as a publisher unless we can synthesize, visualize, and distribute the data to our stakeholders in a way that works for them.

After eight years of use, we have never (and, I hope, would never) made the decision to cease publishing a journal based on Google Analytics data alone. Rather, the data provides us with useful points of entry into conversation with our editors: if a journal falls behind schedule and ceases to communicate, most likely their Google Analytics usage data would reflect this lack of engagement, giving us something to point to in a planning meeting. These metrics are also useful when demonstrating the importance of promoting journals online. Tweets lead to views, and we have the data to prove it! As well, information about which articles were most popular and where in the world readers were coming from equips editors both to justify the value of their journal to others, and to make strategic editorial decisions for the future. While we have also deployed Altmetric across our journals, and made many of the same findings as for books, overall, Google Analytics in combination with Google Data Studio has been the most valuable tool over the long term for gathering and communicating information to others about the usage, reach and – potentially – impact of our journals. It is worth noting, however, that our deep engagement with Google Analytics (configuring it to capture relevant information in our publishing platform, developing custom reports, etc.) is only possible because we host our journals on our own platform. For publishers using a third-party host, this type of customized configuration might not be possible. Since we plan to continue hosting our own journals indefinitely – and to offer a hosting service to other library publishers – we hope that Google Analytics and Google Data Studio reports may inform or even be incorporated into our offering in a way that sets us apart from other online publishing solutions.

Deep Blue

Like most institutional repositories, Deep Blue occupies a position of tension in the scholarly publishing landscape. On one hand, it is directly engaged with and connected to "traditional" modes of publishing, while also pushing back against some of their constraints, by preserving and making openly available versions of research published in scholarly journals. On the other hand, the repository makes possible the publication and preservation of any number of new forms of scholarly output, from slide decks to video recordings of performances to research reports and other forms of gray literature – anything a researcher cares to deposit. At the end of 2018, Deep Blue contained more than 121,000 objects. Of these, approximately one-third have not been published anywhere else, which means that Deep Blue is both preserving and providing worldwide access to more than 40,000 scholarly objects that otherwise would very likely be difficult to find – or not available at all.

Compliance

Of course, if one-third of items in Deep Blue are unique to that platform, the other two-thirds have indeed been published elsewhere, including very often in major scholarly journals. This means that, for many of the articles in Deep Blue, traditional bibliometrics such as a JIF for the journal in which the article was originally published or a citation count for the article may well be available – though the reader would have to visit a third-party index, or perhaps the publisher website, not the Deep Blue interface, to find that information. The copy of a work in Deep Blue is removed from the original context of its publication. This is a good thing for preservation and access; indeed, it is the whole point of the repository: if the original publication is hosted on a publisher website behind a paywall, depositing a version in our own repository allows us to ensure that version remains online, and to expose it to Google and other systems, enabling wider discovery. However, this loss of context makes it difficult for researchers understand the role that Deep Blue plays in increasing the impact of their scholarly portfolio. When it comes time to tell stories of impact, a publication out of context can be an invisible publication, and that is a problem. That is why, as of 2018, work is ongoing to integrate Deep Blue with U-M's research information management (RIM) system, called Michigan Research Experts. Integrating these systems will provide several concrete outcomes: first, it will ensure that all Deep Blue objects are represented on an appropriate Michigan Research Experts profile – thus ensuring that *any* output a researcher deemed worthy of deposit in Deep Blue is "counted" in their profile alongside articles pulled in from other sources such as Scopus, WoS, arXiv, etc. At the same time, we will enable deposit to Deep Blue through the Michigan Research Experts interface. In this way, we hope to make it easier and more seamless for researchers to ensure that they have in fact captured a persistent and accessible record for every research output they care about. Finally, as part of this process, there will be a rationalization of the research objects in Deep Blue and those drawn in from other data sources, which may help to re-contextualize Deep Blue deposits in their proper place in the scholarly conversation. We hope that by integrating Deep Blue with Michigan Research Experts, we will make it possible for both non-traditional research outputs *and* deposited copies of traditionally published work to be more visible and better indexed, facilitating the inclusion of these items when researchers calculate and talk about the impact of their work. Such work is important because of the increasing impact of RIM systems on the landscape of higher education. As the results of a recent survey coordinated by global library cooperative OCLC make clear, deployment of such systems is increasing across the world, spreading from regions where central government funding requires universities to closely monitor their faculty's outputs (such as the UK and Australia) to more distributed contexts such as the US (Bryant et al., 2018). As faculty members beyond STEM fields increasingly face evaluation through such systems, it is important that the full range of their outputs (from books to white papers) be included. Since these often lack the electronic identifiers or indexing feeds that populate the main metrics suppliers, there is a real danger of publications in the humanities and social sciences being woefully under-represented.

Defiance

Of course, even if they are visible on a researcher's profile and easy to find, objects like a slide deck, a recording of a performance, or a set of instructional materials do not fit easily into bibliometric calculations that are careful to include only research articles. And so, even when we successfully include a new type of research object into a system like Michigan Research Experts, those objects are still at risk of being ignored if we rely only on citation-based measures of impact to account for their value. That is why in Deep Blue we are especially interested in exploring new ways of talking about impact. As with our monographs and journals, described above, Altmetric for Publishers has been a valuable tool for us to gather information about how folks are engaging with different types of Deep Blue objects on the web – with one major caveat: Altmetric, to its credit, has put a great deal of development effort into rationalizing and reconciling attention to various versions and locations for an article and rolling all of this engagement into a single score of attention. For most purposes, and certainly for researchers, this is a good thing. Indeed, aggregating usage of the same research made available in different places is one of the biggest challenges we face. But it has a downside: because Altmetric has consolidated this attention, we are no longer able to make any reliable claims about whether attention to an article was driven to the version on the publisher website, or the version deposited in Deep Blue. If we could differentiate between the two, we might be able to say something important about the contribution that this repository service makes to worldwide discovery and use of research published by U-M researchers.

So while Altmetric addresses the use case of gathering information about attention to non-traditional research objects, for journal articles, it actually works against our purpose as a library publisher, which is to make the case for the unique importance of the Deep Blue service and platform. What difference does it make that an item is open? Indexed by Google? Findable on the open web? To answer these questions, measures of success for Deep Blue have typically been communicated in terms of:

(1) The number of items in the repository, which serves as a proxy for comprehensiveness (how close are we to representing the full scholarly output of the university) as well as for value to the campus.

(2) The number of downloads per item. This metric is typically of interest to users at the individual level, and monthly download reports are provided by the system via email to help depositors track how frequently their deposits are being used. For authors, this may serve as a proxy for the value of the research object to users. It might also serve to communicate the value of *open access* to that object or, to put it another way, the particular value of that object to users who might not be able to access it through other channels (i.e., members of the public, or international users, who do not have access to the item through an academic library subscription of their own).

While it is just one repository, because Deep Blue is home to so many different kinds of scholarship, it serves different needs, and contributes to the overall story of a research output, different ways at different times. There are many objects in Deep Blue that will never be captured or counted by other indexes or databases. In those cases, Deep Blue makes a truly unique contribution by capturing some information – via Altmetric and via download counts – about the ongoing value of that object. For research formally published in traditional journals, by assessing usage data available from Altmetric, we may be less interested in making a case for the impact of that scholarly work in and of itself, and rather use the data available to us in a different way to make a case for the unique additional value that the Deep Blue platform and service make possible. Even within a single repository owned and operated entirely within the U-M Library, the purpose of and requirements for scholarly metrics vary widely.

Leading for Change in Our Industry

University presses, committed to producing and delivering the highest quality scholarship even if it is for a small, niche market, are adapting the ways that they work to survive and thrive in a space where revenue from the sale of specialist monographs continues to fall. Michigan Publishing and its peers are evolving rapidly on the fly to respond to and stay ahead of this changing environment. In this process, we are focusing on developing new business models for disseminating our publications; on supporting new, community-developed digital publishing infrastructure; and on cooperating with our peer presses to develop new standards for shared best practices. Research impact metrics have a central role to play in all three areas.

New Business Models

One trend that we see is the organizational movement of presses into libraries. At Michigan Publishing, this was at first a nominal change that helped us to change the narrative surrounding our press on campus from a sales-driven business to a core activity serving the university's mission. In 2014, the U-M Press's transition away from an auxiliary unit of the university to a designated unit in the university's financial structure confirmed that way of thinking, moving the way in which the success of the unit is judged from a focus on revenue to an emphasis on accomplishment of academic mission. The operations and work of our press are not fully funded by the university's general budget – on the contrary, we must recover a substantial portion of the costs of doing business and production in order to keep our doors open. But Michigan Publishing is aligned more closely with the rest of the library, and with any other academic center or institute, than with revenue-generating business like food services or parking. In addition to generating income, then, we are also always looking for ways to communicate the message that Michigan Publishing has a significant impact on our campus and on the world. Stories of impact help us to secure and strengthen our position on campus. In addition to finding new ways to relate to our campus community and administration, we are constantly on the lookout for new ways to reach and make a difference to our authors and our readers. While in many ways we cannot compete with huge commercial publishers, we are also always looking for ways to gain an edge, to be ready to serve new types of author, reader, and institution.

One of the most important business decisions that university presses face as they seek to demonstrate value to their home institutions, comply with the requirements of funding agencies, appeal to an international community of authors and readers, and remain fiscally viable, is how they will respond to the opportunity and challenge posed by OA monograph publishing. In this experimental space, metrics play a particularly important role. At this time, we are especially interested in understanding how OA monographs perform alongside their closed-access siblings; in reporting to funders and administrators what difference has been made by their investment in OA; and in supplying authors with meaningful information about the use of their books in an environment where sales numbers do not provide a full picture. Ultimately, we want to ensure that no matter how we publish a book that it it can reach the same audience, and that we can gather and analyze the same information about its use, so we are not penned in by the limitations of specific programs or platforms in telling a coherent story about the use and impact of *all* of our books.

The OA movement has had a huge impact on scholarly publishing, although the effects have been delayed in the monograph publishing space. Business models that will support OA for monographs, and mandates that require it, are only beginning to emerge. As pressure increases to produce OA monographs, a great deal of research has gone into understanding how much, exactly, it costs to produce a monograph, and what it would take to offset those costs at the point of publication, rather than recovering costs through sales. This would, in theory, relieve the pressure to sell the book and make it possible for the press to sustain its labor while giving the content away. According to a report published by Ithaka S&R in 2016, the "average basic cost" of publishing a scholarly monograph at a public university like Michigan was $28,090 (Maron, Mulhern, Rossman, & Schmelzinger, 2016). How to cover that cost, though, is right now a wildly exploratory environment, with a variety of private and public, collaborative and independent, variously funded programs, initiatives, and models. Of these, the U-M Press has participated in Knowledge Unlatched, through which publishers receive funds (paid by a consortium of participating libraries) to offset the costs of making a selected set of books OA; the NEH/Mellon funded Open Ebook project, which provides grant funding to support publishers in making a set of monographs OA, and the TOME project (described above), along with publishing other OA titles made available on a case-by-case basis, with the result that Michigan Publishing now offers open versions of more than 750 monographs (most of these as part of the U-M Press collection in Hathi Trust), with more published each year.

Community-owned Infrastructure

One of the biggest challenges for Michigan Publishing as we seek to better understand the impact of our publications is simply the extent to which all of these data are owned and managed by third parties, many of whom are unable or unwilling to share the full data in usable ways. Michigan Publishing is in the process of launching a platform for publishing born-digital scholarship: Fulcrum. We know that Fulcrum titles will likely not be well indexed on other platforms in their native form. We also anticipate that many of the titles published on the Fulcrum platform will be the products of new business models, from Knowledge Unlatched to TOME and beyond. Therefore, we recognize that for community-owned infrastructure to succeed, we must account for ways of measuring and communicating meaningful messages about impact for our stakeholders. In 2019, developing robust usage data and reporting mechanisms are a high priority for the Fulcrum developers. Each item in Fulcrum will have a "stats" tab showing a variety of information about the object, including views and altmetrics. Eventually we would like to have dynamic visualizations including geographic maps of usage and more. Our goal is that attractive, straightforward, usable feedback on the impact of the publication will be one of the selling points of our platform – that we will be able to offer an improvement on the data that are currently available to publishers, authors, and readers.

Leadership and Collaboration

It feels like we are at a moment of both great challenge and great opportunity for university presses and library publishers as we seek to position ourselves as a first-choice publishing option for researchers, to respond to the requirements of new and old stakeholders, and to find a place for ourselves in a rapidly changing landscape dominated by large commercial players. We can't do it alone. There is more need than ever for university presses – often competing with one another for authors and titles – to cooperate on issues pertaining to metrics, impact, usage data, publishing platforms, and more. Michigan Publishing seeks out every opportunity to collaborate with our peers in the region (we are lucky to be one of three university presses in the state of Michigan – the only state with such a claim to fame), in the Association of University Presses community, and with international presses who share our values and approach to innovation.

One example of collaboration around metrics is the "Open Access Ebook Usage: Toward a Common Framework" project, for which Michigan Publishing is one of the leads, alongside University of North Texas Library, the Book Industry Study Group, KU Research, and the Educopia Foundation. This initiative, supported by the Andrew W. Mellon Foundation, is exploring the opportunity of creating a collaborative "usage data trust" for open access ebook information. The "data trust" framework is well known in other industries where actual and potential competitors contribute their data in a common pool, administered under agreed governance rules, and are able to extract aggregated insights in return. Recognizing that one of the central challenges of establishing the impact of an open access ebook title is that information is spread across a wide range of publisher and aggregator platforms, the project has been investigating the feasibility of establishing such a framework during 2018 and 2019. Several university presses are involved in the core group, but this also includes commercial book aggregators and publishers as well as standards bodies and researchers from Europe, Australia, and North America.

Future Directions

As the title of this chapter indicates, assessing the impact of the research that we publish has been an interest of Michigan Publishing's since the inception of our organization, but we still consider ourselves to be early in exploring how best to engage with what has been recognized as a data deluge and "metrics tide." As we look to the future, a commitment to taking a critical perspective on what we measure that aligns with our organizational aims and culture is key. As well as ensuring that our publications show up in places where they can be counted by others ("compliance"), we must be focused on interrogating the assumptions behind current modes of research assessment and potentially defining new ways of counting ("defiance").

In terms of "compliance," it is clear that we must ensure that the works we produce leverage persistent electronic identifiers. For a number of years, Michigan Publishing has been a member of CrossRef and has assigned DOIs to its publications. This has been at the level of the article for journals but is currently only at the level of the "work" for books. Adapting our book workflows to assign DOIs to chapters is an immediate priority, while exploring how best to include emerging forms of multimedia-enriched scholarly work in the ecosystem defined by CrossRef and DataCite is an emerging field of challenge and opportunity. Associating works with their authors is another important direction, requiring that we encourage all our authors to create ORCIDs that we can then embed in DOI metadata. At U-M, a workflow has been created that enables researchers to easily associate ORCIDs with their U-M IDs and graduate students submitting dissertations are required to have an ORCID. However, ultimately we can only encourage our authors, since ORCIDs can only now be minted by the researchers themselves.

In terms of "defiance," a questioning attitude to the biases of what is being measured, and how, must be an important aspect of our work. There is a growing movement in the humanities and qualitative social sciences that questions the imposition of value systems created in the STEM fields on disciplines that have developed very differently. The HuMetricsHSS (2017) initiative is aiming to rethink humane indicators of excellence in the humanities and social sciences (HSS), with a focus on establishing a community consensus around values that are essential to all HSS disciplines and that would therefore be appropriate for the development of aligned measures of impact. While seeking new machine-measurable indicators uniquely attuned to HSS disciplines is an element of this project, educating faculty and administrators on how existing measures (such as altmetrics) can be understood in a more nuanced way is perhaps its most productive contribution. HuMetricsHSS aligns with a number of other initiatives focused on responsible use of metrics, committed to by signatories to the San Francisco *Declaration on Research Assessment* (DORA, 2012) and exemplified in tools such as the *Metrics Toolkit* (Metrics Toolkit, 2018).

Research impact metrics as they currently exist and are used are not a natural fit for most of the work that we do at Michigan Publishing. Trying to use them to understand and communicate our publications has often been a struggle – even producing the data is sometimes more work than seems worth it! However, this business is changing rapidly at the same time that our own press, and scholarly publishing more broadly, is also reinventing itself. Informed by some of our research and experiments over the last couple of years, and guided by our current collaborative efforts to lead in this space, we expect that the research impact landscape for university presses and other scholarly publishers in the humanities and social sciences will look dramatically different – and, we hope, meet the evolving needs of authors, institutions, and funding agencies – in a few years' time.

References

About – Michigan Publishing. (2017). https://www.publishing.umich.edu/about/

Bryant, R., Clements, A., de Castro, P., Cantrell, J., Dortmund, A. Fransen, J.Gallagher, P., & Mennielli, M. (2018). *Practices and patterns in research information management: Findings from a global survey*. Dublin, OH: OCLC Research. https://doi-org.proxy.lib.umich.edu/10.25333/BGFG-D241

Dimensions. (2018). https://www.dimensions.ai/info/dimensions-interlinked/

DORA. (2012). https://sfdora.org/

Elsevier Announces its Scopus Book Titles Expansion Program. (2013, October 8). https://www.elsevier.com/about/press-releases/science-and-technology/elsevier-announces-its-scopus-book-titles-expansion-program

HuMetricsHss Humane Metrics Initiative. (2017). https://humetricshss.org/

Mapping the Free Ebook Supply Chain. (2017). https://www.publishing.umich.edu/projects/mapping-the-free-ebook/

Maron, N. L., Mulhern, C., Rossman, D., & Schmelzinger, K. (2016, February 5). The costs of publishing monographs: Toward a transparent methodology. DOI:10.18665/sr.276785

McKenzie, L. (2018, October 18). Closing the gap between university presses and libraries. https://www.insidehighered.com/news/2018/10/18/university-presses-take-control-ebook-distribution

Metrics Toolkit. (2018). http://www.metrics-toolkit.org/

Participating Colleges and Universities. (2018). https://www-arl-org./focus-areas/scholarly-communication/toward-an-open-monograph-ecosystem/current-participants#

Publications. (2017). https://www.publishing.umich.edu/publications/

Ruff, C. (2016, March 22). Academic publishers experiment with 'Altmetrics' to track research and impact. Retrieved from https://www-chronicle-com.proxy.lib.umich.edu/article/Academic-Publishers-Experiment/235785

Watkinson, C., Welzenbach, R., Hellman, E., & Gatti, R. (2017). Mapping the free eBook supply chain: Final report to the Andrew W. Mellon Foundation. https://deepblue.lib.umich.edu/handle/2027.42/137638

Chapter 6

Altmetrics in the Museum Environment

Richard P. Hulser

Introduction

Museums conduct original research and publish in peer-reviewed journals similar to academic institutions but have a focus on outreach and education. Availability of information online provides an opportunity to expand awareness and interaction with museum scholarly research. Altmetrics provide a way to measure attention to museum research activities and use that information to support their work, demonstrate outreach with metrics, and be useful for future planning and programing. This chapter provides an overview of a proof of concept project to examine applicability and usefulness of altmetrics for tracking attention to published research by museum staff and affiliated research associates. The perspectives on altmetrics are outlined from the viewpoint of the institution and of a museum researcher.

Altmetrics in the Museum Environment

Museums are dedicated to the preservation and interpretation of primary evidence of humankind and the environment. Materials are mainly unique and removed from their original context (Lewis, 2018). They are diverse in subject treatment including anthropology, art, history, natural history, and science. Museums have evolved over time from displaying artifacts as curiosities to developing educational programing to enhance the visitor experience. Descriptive information was added to individual and groups of artifacts to help understand why these items were of interest and importance. This involved research to ensure accuracy of information as well as expand knowledge about the artifacts. Research has also been documented through scholarly lectures and publications. Increased worldwide access to information about artifacts is possible in many ways through online published research and discussions. That is why visitor experiences are a key focus for museums whether online or in person. Johnson, Adams Becker, Estrada, and Freeman (2015a, 2015b) note that museums are increasingly focused on capturing and mining data to better understand an audience's interests and needs and offer more focused information on collections (p. 12). Analyzing information about awareness and interest in museum research is a component of that ongoing activity. Museums are similar to academic research institutions. They have departments that do extensive investigations throughout the world and publish the results in peer-reviewed publications. A key difference is research departments in museums need to increase the visibility, understanding, and value of their work beyond discipline and institution. It is important to demonstrate how primary research conducted by staff and affiliated academic associates increases perception of the institution's value to trustees, donors, funding agencies, and the public. Online access can be advantageous as it enables new ways to provide information about collections and activities as well as promote programs and other events. Additionally, online "visits" and interactions are trackable thus providing highly useful metrics that can back up statements and reasoning and be used for program and strategy planning. At the same time, increasing online access to information presents challenges for attention, especially to museums that typically rely on people visiting their physical locations as one of the key ways to show their relevance and attain revenue.

General museum online interactions can be tracked using a variety of analytic tools. So too can attention to research through citation analysis and with the recent advent of altmetrics tools. Citation counts and Journal Impact Factors (JIFs) have been around and used for a long time to provide some explanation of awareness and utility of published research. New tools have since been developed to capture metrics on scholarly impact on the social web (Priem & Hemminger, 2010; Priem, Taraborelli, Groth, & Neylon, 2010). The public uses social media to share information about many activities. Researchers are increasingly using blogs and other social media to expand awareness of ongoing experiments and expeditions including content such as photos, videos, and live broadcasts from their laboratory or field location to show their progress and interact with their audience. This generates public interest while the researchers also work on publishing scholarly articles in more traditional peer-reviewed journals both in print and online. Altmetrics and other new tools are proving useful in measuring online attention to formal research, including through social media. Such tools can aid researchers and their institutions to provide evidence of attention to their work.

Altmetrics tools were not used in museums until around 2014 (Hulser, 2016). The use of altmetrics in academic research environments has been discussed by a number of researchers (Liu & Adie, 2015; Rodgers & Barbrow, 2013; Roemer & Borchardt, 2013). They are useful in other types of research institutions as well, especially museums. The research environment in a museum is typically small compared to that of an academic institution. Scholarly research is done in a number of museums and that work is often published in peer-reviewed print and online journals. Bornmann (2014) and Kwok (2013) discuss a number of reasons why altmetrics are useful to support documentation of scholarly research activities. The expanded and increased recognition of the interest and value of research not seen in traditional literature is particularly applicable to museums. Such institutions are strongly focused on visitors; therefore, the non-traditional sources of information, such as online content and social media, are of high interest. In addition, the fast turnaround time to measure attention in social media is of great value compared to the long amount of time that may be required to get citation counts and other assessments of scholarly work. Therefore, altmetrics tools can be as useful to museums and their research staff as they have long been to academic institutions.

This chapter shows the value of altmetrics through a discussion of a case study of an implementation at a museum with the librarian as the lead project manager.

Altmetrics Use at a Museum

The vision and mission of the Natural History Museum of Los Angeles County (NHMLAC) is "To inspire wonder, discovery, and responsibility for our natural and cultural worlds" (Mission, 2010). The museum has exhibits, many educational programs, and other activities including a variety of ongoing primary research. As with many similar institutions, it is important that activities and research are made known to the largest audience through whatever means possible including onsite activities as well as online interactions. Museum scientists, historians, and other researchers disseminate their findings to professional colleagues through scholarly publications but also participate in educational programs with visitors. Visitors include a variety of people. School groups are a significant portion of the population of visitors to museums in addition to the general public. Scholars and other experts are an additional segment of the visitor population. They spend days or months using museum resources at a deeper level and some collaborate in projects with research staff that are often documented in journal articles and other scholarly output.

Academic institutions typically subscribe to a variety of abstract and citation databases for finding research articles and other contents in subject disciplines in addition to using tools such as Google Scholar. Citation information of publications by academic research staff can more readily be downloadable into bibliographic management and other tools for access by individual researchers as needed. Keeping track of the latest published articles and books is important for museum research departments. This information is typically gathered on a monthly or other periodic basis and reported to senior management to show documented results on research projects. Museums typically, however, do not have a large research staff and student population to justify the expense of licensing abstract and citation databases. Therefore, managing bibliographic citations of scholarly publications is generally an internal staff-intensive process. However, museum research departments also keep track of presentations at professional meetings, interviews with reporters from print and online media companies, and related interactions.

In an effort to help the NHMLAC research department staff reduce the time and effort to compile and manage bibliographic information, possible software tool options that already existed were investigated at library and information sciences conferences. As the investigation of tools proceeded, it was determined that this would solve the management of traditional bibliographic information. It was during this investigation that altmetric applications were discovered that could help with compiling, tracking, and analyzing online sources. Since this was around 2013, altmetrics tools were still new, limited in options available, and not widely known.

Altmetrics tools provide metrics of mentions at the article level. This is more specific than the well-known JIF that is associated with comparing citations in a subject field at the journal title level. As a result, the altmetrics would potentially provide additional and more precise information about interest in a published article.

After information was gathered on available altmetrics tools, an analysis was required to determine whether these were applicable to the needs at the museum. The tool from Altmetric.com compiles data about scholarly research from a number of different online sources such as news media, Wikipedia, Twitter, policy documents, and more, so it can be a one-stop source for more granular attention data among those sources. A sample search for research articles by museum staff was conducted using Altmetric Explorer, and it provided some useful results. In addition to tracking staff contributions to scholarly publications, awareness of mentions of research activities in media and social media were compiled in collaboration with the museum's communications department. The communications department subscribed to an online search tool that provided data on coverage of topics related to the museum. It saved the department time and effort to compile such information. This tool focused on general media and did not pick up information about articles found in research publications, whereas a sample search using the Altmetric tool did so. It was determined that using both tools would be useful as there was little overlap in results.

Detailed information about attention to articles by researchers across the entire department and people affiliated with the museum was obtained in a consolidated way through the use of *Altmetric for Institutions (AFI)*. As this was added functionality, it required a subscription license. Since the initial searches looked promising, a license for AFI was obtained for the purposes of the project. The objective was to determine what data could be obtained and its value and relevance that could be useful at the institutional and researcher levels. The scholarly analytics proof of concept project at NHMLAC was conducted between October 2014 and June 2018. The librarian at the museum was the project lead in a team effort and coordinated activities with the Research and Collections Department office staff and other departments throughout the project. The office staff were already compiling citation information about latest articles published by museum staff and affiliated researchers in academic institutions as well as any interviews with media reporters, external lectures, and other public interactions. It made sense to use this same workflow to gather the necessary information for Altmetric in a consistent and timely manner to eventually provide results. Citations for research papers published by museum staff from 2011 to date were entered into a spreadsheet and sent to the Altmetric office for data entry. Monthly research department meetings at the museum included review and discussions of the most recent scholarly publications, interviews on broadcast news media, and presentations at professional conferences. This information was gathered and consolidated on a regular basis and tracked over time. The resulting metrics were used to demonstrate progress on projects as well as outreach to audiences through reports to senior management, funding agencies, and others as needed. In addition, other content made available online, such as research datasets, would be useful to track. In addition to bibliographic citation information, a digital object identifier (DOI) or similar identifier was required in order to effectively track articles. This was easy enough for those articles in major publications. The challenge was that articles by museum researchers often appeared in journals published by small societies that do not assign such identifiers. This limited the ability for the AFI tool to track mentions of those articles. In addition, the museum's own peer-reviewed research publication *Contributions in Science* historically did not assign a DOI so those articles could not be tracked for this project. A majority of articles in that publication were authored by researchers associated with the museum, so that was a limitation. Thus, the broader challenge of using current altmetrics tools is the need to assign a DOI or other identifier for content produced by an institution. This is additional work with necessary fees in order to be tracked. However, this can be of value in the long run. For example, the United Kindgom's Natural History Museum assigned a unique identifier (DOI) to datasets before making them available online. According to Rees (2017), the reasoning was that it made it easier to track the influence and reach of the content.

Institution View

It is important for a museum as well as the research unit within it to show value of its activities to funding sources and the communities served. Having data to support statements of value strengthens that ability. Such data also help in determining future projects and program development. Museums concentrate on what makes that institution unique or significant to visit and explore in comparison to similar institutions elsewhere, under the umbrella of their core mission. They create and publicize programs with a focus to increase awareness and participation in activities for long-term viability and sustainability of their institution.

Having a tool that consolidates outputs from all staff and affiliated researchers saves time and effort in pulling that information for each individual. Altmetrics tools provide color-coded graphics in addition to tabular data, making it easier to review the results. The AFI tool requires a subscription fee, but it saves time and effort in compiling data for a specific institution and also provides additional functions for reviewing data across departments, research outputs of individuals within a department, and also a breakdown by journals where research is published.

Museums rely on a variety of funding sources to ensure sustainability. In addition to revenue earned through general and special exhibit entry fees, gift shops, restaurants, and other services, grants and donations through public and private sources are very important. Funding agencies are increasingly requiring proof of broader impact gained from their support. For example, the National Science Foundation (NSF, 2018) in their 2018 *Proposal & Award Policies & Procedures Guide* notes a requirement that the application should "present the intellectual merit and broader impacts of the proposed project clearly and should be prepared with the care and thoroughness of a paper submitted for publication" (pp. 1–4).

The requirement for intellectual merit and broader impacts throughout the guide is evidence of the importance given to proof of broader impact as a co-equal with intellectual merit. "Broader impacts" is explained in more detail (pp. 11–12) including a need for evidence of "increased public scientific literacy and public engagement with science and technology." Many museum programs do this on a regular basis, so there is high value to gathering altmetrics data on such outreach. In addition, organizational support of the broader impacts is further stated as a requirement as well. Use of altmetrics can provide data on previously funded projects to help the institution demonstrate such impact to strengthen the proposal. Altmetrics can also be used within the final report of a funded project to back up statements of intended broad impact.

During the proof of concept project, an summary of research outputs using data sourced from Altmetric displayed graphics with article and publication titles providing a visually appealing and easily decipherable way to see relative rankings of the outputs. An example of the top highlights of the museum research outputs on the Altmetric tool is shown in Fig. 1.

This summary was used to highlight the topics of highest interest at the time. Alternative listings were able to be sorted by Altmetric Attention Score from lowest to highest, publication date newest first or oldest first, or by source such as online news stories, mentions in policy documents, or tweets. They could also be sorted by time period such as mentions in the past day, week, month, or year. This provided a way to parse the mentions by time period and examine what relationship, if any, they had to research programs and other activities by the Museum.

The Altmetric data results could also be displayed as a list or in tiled form. This provided an easy way to see a summary of the articles with the highest interest and in what publication they appeared. The article titles were hyperlinked to their online published location as well. If a donut graphic consisted of many different colors, this indicated mentions in a variety of sources. An example of top museum research outputs with multicolored Altmetric Attention Score donuts is shown in Fig. 2.

On the other hand, if there were only a few colors or perhaps only one color, that indicated a more distinct audience source. This information was determined to be useful for future programing purposes. If mentions mainly appeared in news sources, it was thought that perhaps concentrating on informing people from news services would be more efficient, and additional methods were needed for broader outreach.

Access to a consolidated list of journals where research content was published by affiliated researchers enabled quick and easy understanding of where the institution's research had a presence, especially for items published recently. A set of articles with mentions in a particular journal title was shown in a summary chart of the articles with their color-coded donut graphic representing the sources of mentions ranked from most to least mentions. This was able to be restricted to a set time span as well. A timeline chart with color-coded stacked bars displayed mentions for a specified time period whether a week, month, year, or several years (Fig. 3).

This was useful for assessing mentions of particular research output correlated to programs or other institutional activities.

Altmetrics in the Museum Environment   121

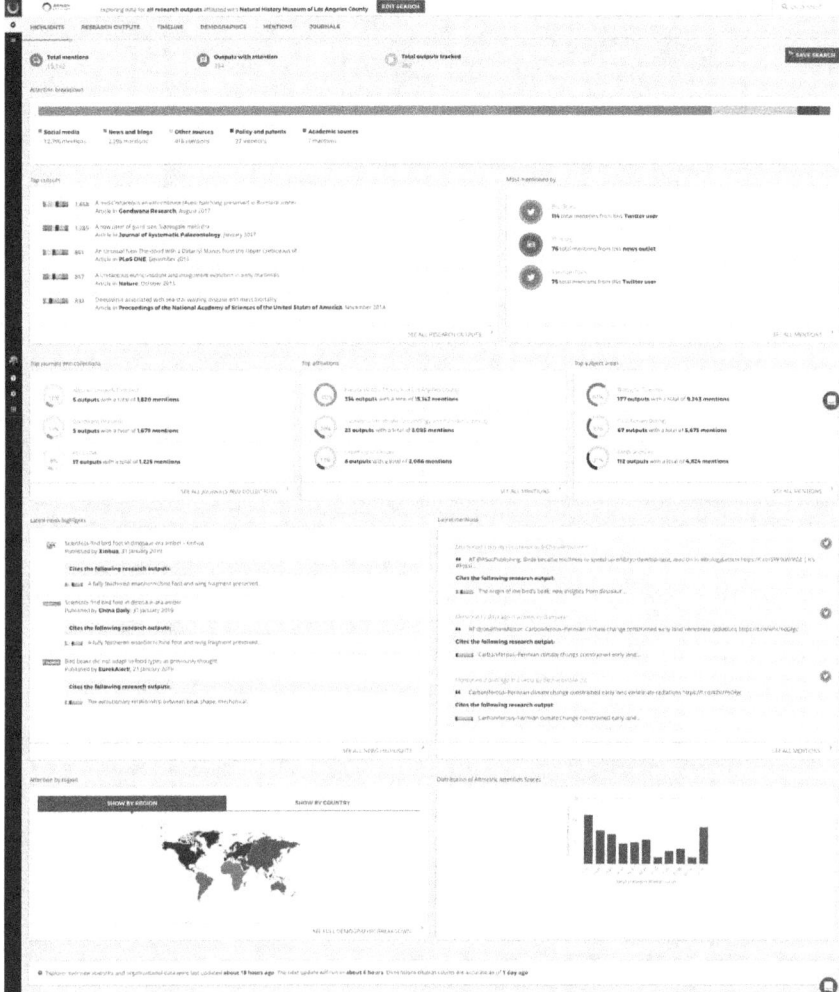

Fig. 1:   Altmetric museum research outputs summary. *(scores and data may have changed since this screenshot was taken on 2/8/19)*

The AFI tool provided additional function and value through the capability to examine a specific institution's research activities. This was of particular interest to the museum executives. Research activities could be further broken down in detail by author, department, journal subject, and custom group. For example, the author tab showed a list of researchers by name along with the number of articles being tracked for each of them. Some authors had multiple articles, and some had many mentions, while others had just a few. It was important to understand

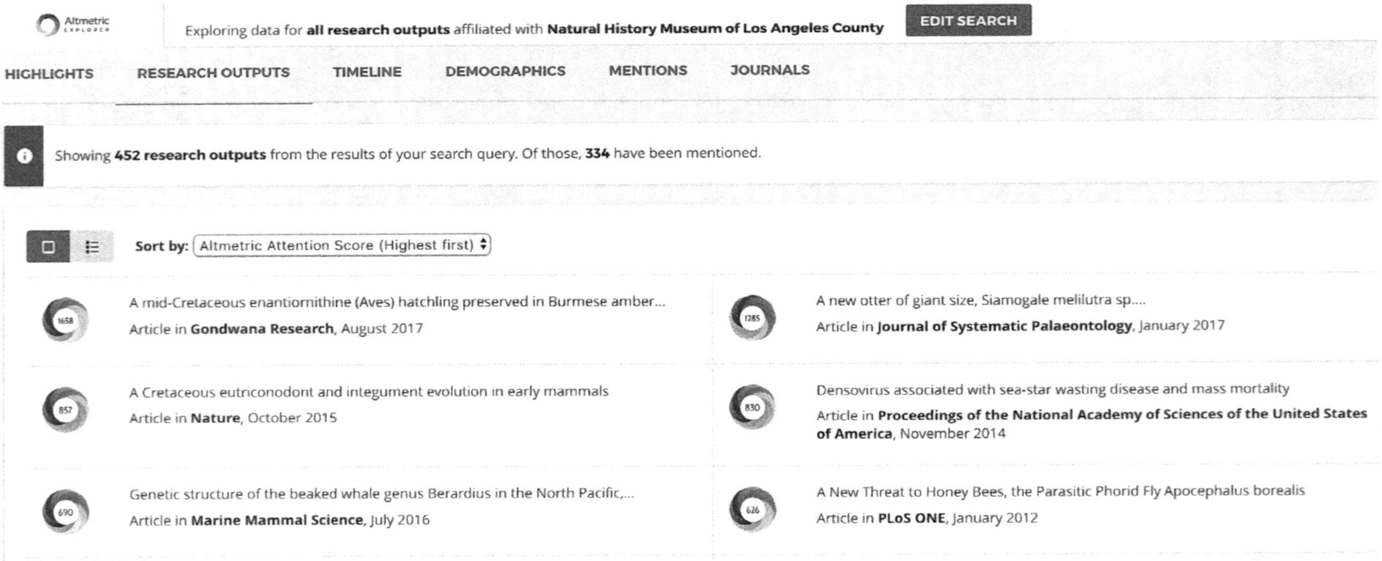

Fig. 2: Top museum research outputs with altmetric attention score donuts. *(scores and data may have changed since this screenshot was taken on 2/8/19)*

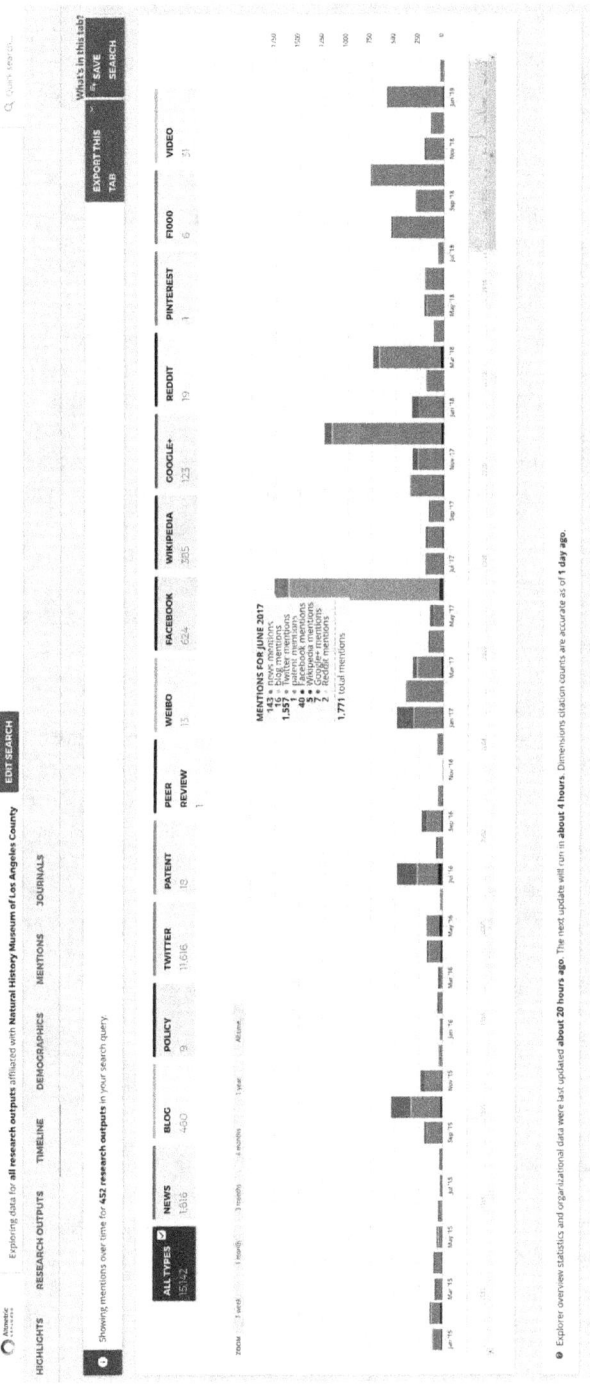

Fig. 3: Altmetric timeline bar chart of museum research outputs spanning January 2015 through February 2019. *(scores and data may have changed since this screenshot was taken on 2/8/19)*

that the number of mentions did not necessarily correlate to the total number of articles published by a particular researcher. For example, one researcher could have 20 articles published with 16 mentions, while another researcher could have 52 articles published with only five mentions. Given that researchers were from a variety of disciplines and fields, comparing one researcher to another solely on this basis was potentially problematic.

Attention paid to the research examined could sometimes be surprising such as a particular research article garnering unexpected attention in online content and social media. For instance, an article about the devastation of sea stars population by a virus was consistently at the top of mentions for the museum for most of the project. While published in 2014, the article was still of strong interest four years later as it appeared in fourth place in November 2018. Sometimes an article may become static in attention only to get renewed significant attention long after it was published. The Altmetric chart over time would easily show this and reasons behind the increased interest could be determined through detailed examination of the social media posts. This was important to both the institution and the researcher as it showed long-term value of the work done.

Further examination of the attention was explored looking at the list showing a headline of a post as well as the originating news outlet. The full original post was reviewed through the hyperlink. This was of value to the museum as it enables the marketing and communications department to determine the source and what was said in the posting about the topic of the article. Some of the news outlet sites displayed icons, data on mentions and shares from that page as well as comments from readers, so it was possible to obtain additional information on tracking besides what was shown in Altmetric.com. A single news outlet was sometimes shown to have a large number of subscribers new and different from those typically reached through press releases and other announcements.

Research staff were responsible for alerting the museum's communications team about a newly published article, so a press release could be issued about it. In one instance, the Altmetric.com results showed a particular research article was getting many mentions although a press release had not yet gone out about the article. This was a surprise and an additional way for the communications team to become aware of a need to create a press release in the future and perhaps include that in reports and presentations.

Researcher View

Altmetrics can be of high value to researchers, especially those in museums who are focused on outreach and want to be able to capture information on how effective their programs and activities are in reaching external audiences. Lessard, Whiffin, and Wild (2017) state the following in their article:

> Social media has the power to promote museum and collection events, research, and staff, as well as raise awareness of entomological collections and demonstrate their relevance to

the public, industry, policy makers, and potential students of entomology. (p. 467)

The challenge is being able to measure this, and that is where altmetrics can be utilized.

The challenge for researchers is to harness social media discussions to enable a better awareness of the extended value of their work. This is important as evidence of broader impacts of research efforts are being required by funding agencies, such as the NSF, and private donors alike. Funders want to ensure the money provided is being used as intended and want to see how research activities have an impact on other researchers, as well as a broader audience. During the period of the proof of concept project, some museum researchers at NHMLAC posted information on blogs and various social media platforms, but capturing this information in a consistent, efficient way was always a challenge. Having an ability to add such information to the scholarly research data already gathered gave a better idea of the broad reach of their work. Again a number of articles by museum researchers were published in journals where no DOI or other unique identifier was assigned by the publisher, so those articles were more difficult or impossible to track by the Altmetric tool.

The Altmetric Explorer tool was capable of displaying a list of research output and the mention activity of each author, thus enabling a researcher to track their own progress and what topics/areas generate mentions and those that do not. This functionality had the potential to help a museum researcher understand what topics might be of particularly high interest. This did not affect research plans but did provide informational guidance for future visitor-related programming. Alternatively, it may show topics that could be of higher interest but currently not generating mentions. Further efforts may be needed by the researcher or communications department to get that research information more widely known.

A key feature of Altmetric was that mention results were "auditable" with a link from the mention directly back to the full original posting in the tracked online sources. This capability enabled further assessment of a mention to determine the origin of the posting and provide possibilities for additional contacts. Mentions in a variety of sources were tracked by Altmetric and it was helpful to be able to examine each source of mentions for a particular article and how each source found the mentioned article of interest. The mention data would not show whether the interest was positive or negative but linking to the original posting would provide the text and therefore enable assessment of it. Articles with mentions in a broad set of sources were displayed with multiple colored donut graphics with each color or shade of color representing the particular source of a mention. Fig. 4 shows an example of an article with mentions in a variety of sources.

The multiple colors in donuts helped distinguish widely covered mentions from those that had a more focused set of sources that would be displayed with one or just a few colors in the donut graphic. For example, a particular research topic such as a virus affecting bees or subject area such as entomology generated

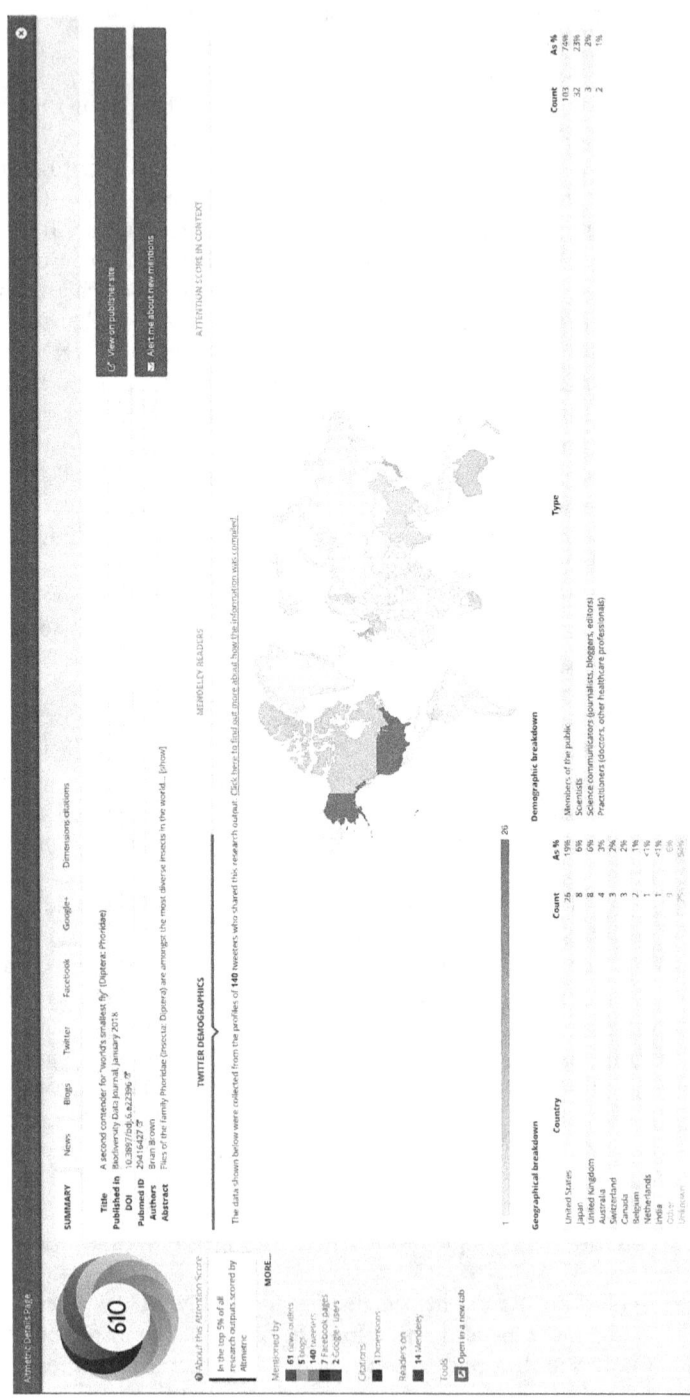

Fig. 4: Research article with multicolor altmetric attention score donut. (*scores and data may have changed since this screenshot was taken on 2/8/19*)

a large amount of mentions on Twitter. This was shown through a predominantly light blue donut. In another case, a topic showed high numbers of mentions in online news sources that were indicated with a predominantly red donut graphic. This enabled a researcher to see what online media were used to comment on the research.

This was of value to museum researchers since they were focused both on their research and also on engaging with their peers and the public. Traditional citations do link back to other articles and seeing those is becoming easier as efforts are made to increase availability of those articles' availability online. However, those links are to referenced items in the published article that are typically months if not years old. Mentions are typically comments that are current and therefore more timely. Mentions also draw from a broader range of sources. If a particular article showed high interest through any mentions mainly in online news, this could cause a researcher to plan on ensuring more information was available through that means in the future to either sustain or broaden outreach in that or other sources.

Researchers mentioned concerns when their article was not of high interest because only a few mentions were noted for it. Further detailed examination was needed to see what those few mentions represented. While they could indeed be posted by just a few specific individuals, one or more of those people turned out to be a well-known scientist or a research journalist who had several hundred followers. The mentions sometimes were from major international news outlets with many thousands of subscribers and thus many more readers of the posting than the initial mention seemed to initially represent. The background of the person or entity originating the mention was able to be discerned and that was extremely helpful in determining the value of a mention.

There was also potential for misinterpretation of the data shown. The perception of a lower number of mentions could make researchers uncomfortable in how those will be interpreted by upper management. There often were differences that showed relatively low numbers of mentions for a research article yet a large presence in general online news media. This caused some confusion on what was really tracked, what was missed, and how to interpret all of it. A lower number did not necessarily mean people were not talking about the research article as it just showed the tracked mentions. While the numbers of mentions were low in a particular instance, this did not represent the quality of the work, the relative importance of any one of the articles in a particular field of research, or other qualitative assessments. Mentions could be positive or negative and the metrics did not reflect either stance. The number listed did not represent anything more than it was a mention. In addition, the mention could be short and concise or quite lengthy, and quality was unknown until read. There was concern by researchers that any institution would use this information to do a compare and contrast of one research department to another when their disciplines, such as entomology and anthropology, were completely different in many ways. A researcher could immediately be concerned because it may appear that with only a few mentions shown in this tool that their article was not of high interest, but that was not necessarily the case.

Altmetrics tools have been around for over eight years. Speakers at the 5:AM Conference in London in 2018 indicated that there is a lot of work needed for altmetrics tools to be more inclusive of more sources from publishers worldwide and in languages other than English (Programme 5: AM Altmetrics Meeting, n.d.). Museum researchers collaborated on projects in various locations worldwide and published in a variety of sources beyond those in English, so there would be increased value if broader coverage by altmetrics tools were available. While international coverage was a work in progress during this project, the Altmetric tool did provide a world map for Twitter mentions with color shading showing the origin of mentions. Tables accompanying the map provided geographic and demographic breakdowns of the mentions as well. If a research output was provided by a publisher based in a specific country such as England or the United States, this was often reflected in the number of mentions appearing from that geographic location.

Mentions in Wikipedia noted through Altmetric.com enabled museum researchers to document where they were seen as a knowledgeable resource on a topic. Being cited in Wikipedia was another way to show how researchers influenced discovery, was seen as an authority on a topic, and supported the broader impact of their work. A cited presence in Wikipedia was a positive point for researchers.

Researchers in museums have similar concerns as their colleagues in academic institutions about use of altmetrics and the measurements of research pursuits. Some administrators at various research institutions were known to be focused on how many articles were published in journals with high impact factors and similar measurements to assess value and productivity of their research staff. Museum researchers indicated it was more important to focus more closely on quality, rather than on quantity or popularity, regardless of their institutional affiliation. They would rather be judged by a proper assessment of the qualitative contribution of their work than such metrics.

Objections noted by Bornmann (2014) were also raised at the museum including manipulation or gaming of the metrics as well as a focus on higher numbers of participants as an important factor and not necessarily the quality of the content or data (pp. 899–900). During the proof of concept project, museum researchers wondered what would stop the creation of additional personas to stack the numbers of mentions in various social media platforms. The discovery since 2016 of large numbers of fake profiles and posts in social media created by "bots" related to elections in the United States and elsewhere are but one example of this concern that could exist with postings about research as well.

Museum researchers were concerned that altmetrics will be yet another metric used to assess the quality of their work and potential for advancement. Such measurements were seen as a way to judge the researchers' short-term popularity of what they do rather than for the fundamental research endeavor. They were concerned that this could affect their career regarding position, advancement, and perception of contribution to the institution and beyond. Their viewpoint was that the research in which they are engaged should be viewed as more important and a significant contribution to knowledge in the long term, regardless of whether it was of expanded interest to the population at large. These comments were brought up in department meetings and the researchers indicated this was a topic at annual meetings of their peers as well.

Summary

Museums focus on preserving collections and expanding awareness, knowledge, and appreciation of the world around us. Original scholarly research is an important component of the activities at many museums. Altmetrics tools provide a way to capture and analyze metrics to demonstrate awareness and appreciation of that research in the online environment. The proof of concept project using the Altmetric tool provided an understanding of attention to research articles beyond traditional citations. It proved of some value to both the institution and to individual researchers. A key feature was the ability to link back to original postings of mentions. Graphical representation through the color-coded donuts and graphic charts provided additional ways to view and analyze the data. The Altmetric tool provided a good baseline for measuring and reporting on museum research output in an online environment. Results of the project provided the communications department additional data and news sources and provided another way to see how research output was tracking with outreach activities. Some researchers became actively involved in monitoring their own research with easy-to-use tools and gained new ways to track and promote their work. The Altmetric tool provided an avenue for researchers to make their own conclusions on how their work was perceived and by whom, whether a peer, a research reporter, or a member of the public.

References

Adams Becker, S., Cummins, M., Davis, A., Freeman, A., Giesinger Hall, C. Ananthanarayanan, V., et al. (2017). *NMC horizon report: 2017 Library edition*. Austin, TX: The New Media Consortium.

Bornmann, L. (2014). Do altmetrics point to the broader impact of research? An overview of benefits and disadvantages of altmetrics. *Journal of Informetrics, 8*(4), 895–903. arxiv.org/abs/1406.7091v2

Freeman, A., Adams Becker, S., Cummins, M., McKelroy, E., & Giesinger, C. (2016). *NMC horizon report: 2016 Museum edition*. Austin, TX: The New Media Consortium.

Hulser, R. P. (2016). *Altmetrics: Social media metrics tools expanding the librarian's role*. arxiv.org/abs/1406.7091v2. DOI:10.6084/m9.figshare.5457289

Johnson, L., Adams Becker, S., Estrada, V., & Freeman, A. (2015a). *NMC horizon report: 2015 library edition*. Austin, TX: The New Media Consortium.

Johnson, L., Adams Becker, S., Estrada, V., & Freeman, A. (2015b). *NMC horizon report: 2015 museum edition*. Austin, TX: The New Media Consortium.

Kwok, R. (2013). Research impact: Altmetrics make their mark. *Nature, 500*(7463), 491–493. DOI:10.1038/nj7463-491a

Lessard, B. D., Whiffin, A. L., & Wild, A. L. (2017). A guide to public engagement for entomological collections and natural history museums in the age of social media. *Annals of the Entomological Society of America, 110*(5), 467–479. DOI:10.1093/aesa/sax058

Lewis, G. D. (2018). Museum. *Encyclopaedia Britannica Online*. Retrieved from https://www.britannica.com/topic/museum-cultural-institution

Liu, J., & Adie, E. (2015). Realizing the potential of altmetrics within institutions, *Ariadne*, 72. http://www.ariadne.ac.uk/issue72/liu-adie

Mission. (2010, May 26). *Natural History Museum of Los Angeles*. https://nhm.org/site/about-our-museums/mission.

National Science Foundation. (2018). Proposal & award policies and procedures guide, NSF 18-1, OMB control number 3145-0058. https://www.nsf.gov/pubs/policydocs/pappg18_1/nsf18_1.pdf

Priem, J. & Hemminger, B. H. (2010), Scientometrics 2.0: New metrics of scholarly impact on the social Web. *First Monday*, 15(7). http://firstmonday.org/ojs/index.php/fm/article/view/2874/2570

Priem, J., Taraborelli, D., Groth, P., & Neylon, C. (2010). Altmetrics: A manifesto. http://altmetrics.org/manifesto

Programme | Altmetrics 5:AM. (n.d.). http://www.altmetricsconference.com/programme/.

Rees, A. (2017). Open data sets at the Natural History Museum. https://www.altmetric.com/blog/open-data-sets-at-the-natural-history-museum/

Rodgers, E. P., & Barbrow, S. (2013). A look at altmetrics and its growing significance to research libraries. http://hdl.handle.net/2027.42/99709

Roemer, R. C., & Borchardt, R. (2013). Institutional altmetrics and academic libraries. *Information Standards Quarterly*, 25(2), 14–19. DOI:10.3789/isqv25no2.2013

Chapter 7

What Have We Learned Today? A Synthesis of Cases Presented

Elaine M. Lasda

The organizations profiled in this work are of diverse origins, structure, and purpose. There are both similarities and differences in their approaches to providing impact metrics services. The cases described also highlight benefits to the library or information center providing services and the parent organization. These cases underscore the best practices that are emerging from various areas of the scientometric, information science, and library communities.

Divergence Across Cases

Range of mission and purpose. Disciplines and missions extending from the advancement of hard science, technology and engineering, education and learning, regulatory enforcement, economic savings, community-supported publishing, and open access scholarship are all represented.

Funding sources of parent organization. A range of revenue sources fund these organizations, including government (both state and Federal, from legislative and agency sources), public and corporate donations, grants, organizational membership fees tuition, publication sales, and subscriptions.

Parent organization activities. While a number of the cases have policymaking or regulatory implications to their mission, public education/programming, communications, and staff development as activities that may be influenced by impact measurements.

Subjects and objects being evaluated. Subjects of evaluation not only include the usual peer-reviewed journal articles (PRJAs), staff researchers/scientists, institutional benchmarks, and other scholarly output but also include equipment use, a cyberinfrastructure, whole projects, and non-scholarly publications.

Impact data output formats. The actual vehicle for which value of research was being demonstrated differed from organization to organization. The final outputs containing the indicators include organizational annual reports, award nominations, specialized "impact statements," spreadsheets, and web pages.

Technical resources and staff skill sets. Resources available to gather impact metrics vary greatly as well as staff strengths and skills. Berkeley's Institute of Transportation Studies (ITS) has a skilled staff using low cost or free resources; in the opinion of this author, Michigan Publishing has both highly skilled staff and an abundance of resources at its disposal. National Center for Atmospheric Research (NCAR) has staff with the ability to build an Application Programming Interface (API) whereas the Environmental Protection Agency (EPA) hopes to recruit intern staff to fill a technical skills role. At the museum, librarians had certain data entry processes performed by the metrics provider.

Maturity and level of services provided. ITS describes a setup process that will facilitate the tracking of gray literature in transportation research going forward. Michigan Publishing has a well-developed suite of metrics for their journal editors and has experimented with many resources to get the best data for their authors and editors. The EPA and NCAR have well-developed programs with plans for growth, and the museum model serves more as a proof-of-concept.

Challenges Across Cases

Despite differing characteristics in many regard, these cases share similar challenges in undertaking projects relating to research impact metrics.

Labor-intensive processes. Despite new tools, gathering metadata on a workable set of scholarly outputs from which to generate indicators was a particular challenge in each case. Much human "massaging" of the retrieved data and resultant analysis was needed to make the content fit for stakeholder consumption. Despite improved analytics in many tools such as Web of Science, Altmetric, and Google products, data cleaning, transformation, display, and interpretation by the libraries and information centers made material relevant and useful to requestors and stakeholders.

Lack of standardized identifiers across output type. Every case presented indicated the loss of some information as a result of a lack of DOIs (or a tool's exclusion of other kinds of persistent identifiers), author identifiers such as ORCID, and other identifiers that would have made it possible to more easily track the dissemination of the research output in question. In some cases, this lack is a greater problem than others. Even in traditional bibliometrics, it is essentially impossible to get to a citation count of "n=all," but improving the trackability of formats such as conference proceedings, gray literature, data, and other non-PRJA scholarly output will benefit the entire research community, regardless of discipline.

"Out of the box" resources not a complete solution. Whether Web of Science/InCites, Altmetric, Google Scholar, or another tool was used, no single tool proved adequate to fully describe research impact beyond providing data for included traditional PRJAs. Web searches, news monitoring, and other creative ways of finding impact help to supplement the data provided by metrics sources. It is challenging to describe the full impact of research topics from sources where the specific output is not attributed. Likewise, demonstrating the reach of a new scientist/researcher's activities can mean going beyond the h-index or other indicators. Certainly the major citation index services have made inroads with regard

to adding content for books, data, conference proceedings, emerging fields, and so forth, and perhaps we will see increasingly more robust and nuanced data from the citation index providers.

The metrics likewise have limitations. As noted elsewhere in this book, just because a metric is capturable does not mean it provides meaningful insights or clarifies understanding of a topic or problem. News hits, human narratives, anecdotes, and context can help, along with human interpretation to complete the picture. Furthermore, some of the issues presented with indicators of research impact are discipline specific; several of the case studies presented here point to the increased need for data to support and describe social science and humanities research impact. Hargens (2000) states that there is a propensity to cite older works in addition to a longer turnaround time in citation count in the social sciences and humanities. He attributes this to a greater need for social scientists to convince others of the validity of their research, given the weak evidence in most social science methodologies. Thus, a researcher traces the lineage of one's line of inquiry through to the great thinkers of yore within the field (in Cronin & Atkins, 2000, p. 511).

Requestors of impact metrics do not always understand the metrics. Within and outside the research domain, the organizations for which metrics are provided often need information and education on the purpose, prevalence, strengths, and limitations of the supplied information.

Demonstrating research impact outside the field. All organizations described an interest in showing impact outside the disciplinary or research domain. This may at times run contrary to attitudes in academia, namely the researcher who feels so long as his or her research is indexed in the "right" places, peers, or others with the same specialization will be able to locate the work; therefore, the researcher need not make efforts to extend discoverability beyond key journals (usually paywalled). While this sentiment is slowly eroding in academia, specialized research entities are perhaps at this time under greater need to demonstrate the value of their work as it is integrated into the fabric of society, and not simply that it has been read or accessed by ivory tower cronies.

Necessity of educating users, or *"metric literacy."* A vital role for the library or information center is instruction on research impact metrics, whether one-on-one as for the journal editors working with Michigan Publishing or through workshops at the EPA. Internal constituencies such as organizational administrators and the researchers themselves often benefit from instruction as well, as with the museum and NCAR. This lack of understanding provides both a challenge and an opportunity to the library or information center providing this information.

Other Examples of Specialized Research Impact Services

It is worth noting other interesting case studies in the published literature that are not included in this work. For example, the National Institute of Standards and Technology is performing topical network analysis, text mining, cluster analysis, and other sophisticated methodologies with their impact data. They are able to map emerging research areas, collaborations, and disciplinary landscapes (Makar & Trost, 2018). The National Institutes of Health's (NIH) Library, long on the cutting edge of providing services related to bibliometrics and research impact, have two informationist staff members who are experts in bibliometrics and research impact. The NIH Library has a user-friendly website and shares knowledge through the Bibliometrics and Research Symposium which they have held twice, bringing together librarians and others who practice these services across disciplinary domains ("Bibliometric Services | NIH Library," n.d.). Librarians at NIH also studied the provision of research evaluation services in seven biomedical libraries (Gutzman et al., 2018). One NIH informationist was embedded in a project analyzing three decades of publications related to obesity under a given grant (Nicastro et al., 2016).

Demonstrating Impact Beyond the PRJA

There are many formats of output that have influence, reach, and impact on scholarly thought than the PRJA. As a result, there are new standards and practices evolving to facilitate the measurement of their impact. Citation of datasets is being studied by a number of scholars. This is a key issue with new public data requirements from funders and publishers (Borghi, Abrams, Lowenberg, Simms, & Chodacki, 2018; Fenner et al., n.d.; Konkiel, 2013; Piwowar, 2011; Robinson-García, Jiménez-Contreras, & Torres-Salinas, 2016; Tenopir et al., 2011). FORCE11 has issued *a Joint Declaration of Data Citation Principles* which recommends best practices for documenting the reuse of datasets. These include: giving data the same weight as PRJA and other scholarly output in terms of legitimacy, facilitating a standard attribution style for datasets, citation of data to back up claims, creation or adoption of persistent identifiers, persistent metadata for discovery and specific description, and interoperability among fields (Data Citation Synthesis Group, 2013). Likewise, FORCE11 has proposed similar best practices for citation of software (Smith, Katz, Niemeyer, & FORCE11 Software Citation Working Group, 2016).

Patents represent another set of challenges in attribution and tracing citations. Such challenges include the differences in citation patterns in international patent offices as well as disciplinary fields, tracking examiner-added citations, and the effects of technology transfer (Alcácer & Gittelman, 2006; Jaffe & de Rassenfosse, 2017; Sorensen & Chambers, 2008).

The reach of non-PRJA research output can sometimes be captured by altmetrics or even Google Scholar, but there are gaps in coverage of many output formats, including but not limited to posters, computational algorithms and modeling, presentation slide decks, recordings, visual arts, and performances. Establishing best practices to measure and determine the true significance or level of influence and impact these outputs garner is a field of emerging study.

Naysayers and Chicken Littles

An increased reliance on metrics of various ilks has led to a proliferation of metrics critics. Is assessment and evaluation through metrics a form of surveillance like Muller posits? Is this a "tyrannical" means of research evaluation (Muller, 2018)?

The reality is that "new" metrics such as altmetrics, usage metrics, web analytics, and the like, when combined with traditional citation-based approaches such as the Journal Impact Factor (JIF), can be paired with expert evaluation and peer review, to provide a nuanced and effective profile for organizations to be able to demonstrate value, allocate resources, and answer questions of direction and focus. Does this result in a loss of autonomy for researchers? Does it engender and encourage the gaming of the research metrics system, leaving us with "bad apples" that spoil the validity and integrity of scholarly metrics as a whole? Does this reliance on the data and benchmarking reward mediocrity over innovation? To what extent have the pressures of the academy bled into other types of research organizations? There are myriad complaints but minimal research or data to back up the concerns expressed by many of the naysayers and chicken littles.

That does not mean that all criticism is without merit. As with any data problem, we need to make certain the data collected and the metrics utilized answer a legitimate and useful question that provides insight and information to the stakeholders to whom the information is presented. Easy to collect and analyze data may not always be the most informative. This is perhaps a significant issue with any sort of data, assessment rubric, or protocol in any field or sector, yet efficient-to-collect data and metrics are all too often used as an expedient proxy for indicators that have real value or worth.

Likewise, it would be foolhardy given the nuanced, multidimensional, and complex nature of the research process to boil down a research unit's effectiveness to a single indicator or score. Take, for example, the *h*-index. Hirsch (2005) may have felt that the panel of citation data provided in an academic dossier may be too complex and confusing for reviewers. Perhaps however, the answer to that criticism is not the creation of a simplistic integer-based indicator, but rather education of evaluators and those who are evaluated, assuring the best of our ability that there is "metric literacy."

Efforts at Regulation

Myriad concerns exist regarding the limitations of research impact metric use, misuse based on lack of understanding, and outright fraud or gamesmanship. Concerns regarding their limitations generally center around the insufficient coverage of relevant literature, a lack of transparency in publication and research sets used to derive the analysis, issues with the statistical methodologies used to calculate a given metric, and so forth. Efforts at raising awareness of misuse issues abound. For example, the San Francisco *Declaration on Research Assessment* is supported by a group of authors and organizations who oppose the use of journal-based metrics (particularly the JIF) for evaluating individual researchers (San Francisco Declaration on Research Assessment (DORA), 2019).

In the UK, the Responsible Use of Metrics movement from which a report called *The Metric Tide* provided recommendations for responsible use. Many of its recommendations apply specifically to the UK *Research Evaluation Framework* and/or to academic institutions, but others are generally applicable, for example, using the term "indicator" over "metric;" calling upon institutions to establish policies and statements in favor of responsible use; educating researchers in the limitations of indicators; making the data and methodologies used transparent to the community; reducing reliance on journal-based measures; promoting identifiers such as ORCID, Interanational Standard Name Identifier (ISNI) and DOIs; and creating community supports, including the website www.ResponsibleMetrics.org (Wilsdon et al., 2015).

Similarly, the *Leiden Manifesto* provides 10 criteria for using research metrics in evaluation. These criteria center around openness; alignment with research mission, including local scope mission; disciplinary contextualization; use of multiple metrics; understanding the limitations of the metrics; transparency of methodology and allowing researcher verification of data; and regular evaluation of the suite of metrics used for assessment and review (Hicks, Wouters, Waltman, de Rijcke, & Rafols, 2015).

In the US, some attention has been paid to the question of best practices related to the use of altmetrics. The National Information Standards Organization (NISO) developed recommendations to standardize altmetrics and identify situations where altmetrics might be effectively utilized. These use cases are framed in terms of eight "personas" of stakeholders and three overarching themes of use. The personas include: librarians, research administrators, hiring committee members, funding agency staff, academics/researchers, publishers/editors, media/journalists, public information officers, and content platform providers. The overarching themes where altmetrics might be deemed applicable are: the demonstration of scholarly achievement, the assessment of "impact or reach" of research, and increasing the discoverability/findability of scholarship and researchers (National Information Standards Organization, 2016, pp. 1–3).

Best Practices

To generate an appropriate dashboard or "impact statement" for a given research entity, we need to ask first and foremost, what is the mission of that entity? In this book we have seen five considerably different goals and missions of the organizations presented. How does the use of research impact metrics further an organization's mission? What is the organization trying to demonstrate and how is it best described? It is imperative for the compiler to have a clear understanding of the mission, vision, goals, and objectives of their organization. This will ensure the service is of the most possible value to the parent organization. Specialized organizations can be an example for the slower-moving higher educational institutions which rely heavily on traditional bibliometric indicators related to PRJAs. A research entity not focused on promotion and tenure dossiers may have the ability to be more flexible in choosing what to measure, how to analyze and visualize it. There is no one right or wrong way to accomplish this, but as we have seen, the need to take care to carry out this undertaking responsibly has been demonstrated by the cases contained herein. Specialized information centers and libraries have the ability to be role models in the responsible use of the metrics movement.

Benefits for the Library or Information Center

There are many benefits to the specialized library or information center which provides research impact metrics services to its parent organization. These are not really any different than the benefits gleaned by academic libraries for providing the same services; however, because their expenses are often perceived as overhead (read: source for cutting), specialized libraries can be under a measurably greater need to demonstrate their value and relevance to their parent organization. Collaboration with researchers, administrators, and other internal stakeholders and constituencies is a valuable byproduct from meeting research impact data needs that engenders greater visibility for the library. As the expertise of librarians and information professionals is recognized, they may be asked to partner on other projects, even becoming "embedded" in a given team or organization undertaking (Shumaker & Talley, 2009). Providing needed support for mission-critical activities of the parent organization can only broaden the portfolios of valuable and relevant services recognized by leaders and administrators and may engender new library/information center champions. Finally, the improved educational prospect of "metric literacy" in organizations bolsters the research ecosystem as a whole: "a rising tide raises all ships."

Benefits for the Greater Organization

Improved confidence in the numbers. Research impact indicators do not have to exist in a vacuum. Strengths and limitations are contextualized by librarians/information professionals. The parent organization can go forward with greater confidence and understanding of its reach and impact.

The law of comparative advantage. Let each party focus on what they do best: scientists as scientists, administrators as administrators, letting the impact metrics experts lead the way in understanding how indicators are best utilized. To maximize the law of comparative advantage, however, each party must communicate and exchange the benefit of their own expertise. The domain expert and the metrics expert work together to create a better-informed and contextualized picture of the research landscape of the parent organization.

Better communication. Researchers and organizations are likewise better able to communicate their reach and from that make decisions, allocate resources, receive awards, goals, and objectives.

Own the story. Armed with a new understanding and ability to communicate influence and impact, these services give the parent organization an opportunity to change the narrative, to "own" the metrics, decide how to tell its own story.

So What are the "New" Metrics?

The case studies presented in this volume utilize a variety of bibliometric, altmetric, and other indicators from which to create an understanding of research impact for various types of research units and their requisite research outputs.

Judging by these five examples, there is still heavy reliance on traditional bibliometric indicators as a measure of scholarly research output. Particularly beyond simple citation counts, Web of Science's JIF remains nearly ubiquitous in the analyses presented, albeit for divergent purposes. While there are many newer bibliometric indicators, those provided by Web of Science still hold their place as the gold standard for measurement. Many newer indicators—Eigenfactor, Source Normalized Impact per Paper, SCImago Journal Rank, CiteScore, i10, and others—are understood by information scientists, scientometricans, librarians, and other bibliometrics experts, but it is likely they are not well understood by non-specialists. The one newer metric that seems to have permeated the non-specialist mentality is the h-index, which is of questionable merit as an evaluative tool, as has been noted earlier in this work.

Many of the cases presented here use metrics other than bibliometric or altmetric indicators as a barometer for the impact of the scholarly output they are tracking. Usage metrics, costs, and components of altmetric indicators such as news hits or social media mentions may be the "new" metrics. Really though, the term "new metrics" could be considered a misnomer. In this rapidly evolving field, what one might consider "new" metrics are not yet widely adopted. Is this changing? The rate at which they are adopted lags significantly behind newer analytics development.

Bigger, cheaper, faster data and analytics could bring further changes in demonstrating future research impact. It is highly doubtful given the current science policy climate that there will be an increase in the proportion of Federal government funds spent on R&D projects, and a plateau or decrease will likely be reflected in other funding sources. Increase in scholarly output, both in terms of content and format, combined with fewer funds will only lead to escalating demand for accountability on the part of the research unit. Demonstrating the value of research has moved beyond the scholarly PRJA and the academy.

The future and the landscape of research impact metrics, with its manifestos, declarations, and report recommendations, have a solid grounding from which to continue to improve. There is ample signage pointing the way down the path to a more informative and useful suite of indicators, data tools, and analysis methodologies to show new relations between researchers, research fields, and research output. Linked data sources such as Dimensions may give us the power to see more nuanced levels of reach and impact at various stages of the research cycle. To those who say this is surveillance and by subtext oppressive, data collection and tracking is a juggernaut in all fields these days. Trying to undo all of the data collection that is being undertaken with regard to research and other sections would be like trying to put toothpaste back in the tube. Clearly, in fields far beyond research evaluation the many benefits of having more data available has transcended concerns of surveillance, privacy intrusion, and so forth. What we must strive for is implementation of best practices akin to those discussed here and elsewhere. An important practice to make ubiquitous is transparency of data collection and methodology. Self-ownership and/or access to data about a subject and how it is being used, likewise is powerful in its own right. Those who have concerns about misuse, fraud or other aspects of data-driven decision-making as regards research evaluation should be encouraged to continue to bring critiques before the arena of public and scientific discourse where there can be an iterative process of continuous research evaluation improvement and refinement.

References

Alcácer, J., & Gittelman, M. (2006). Patent Citations as a Measure of Knowledge Flows: The Influence of Examiner Citations. *The Review of Economics and Statistics*, *88*(4), 774–779. DOI:10.1162/rest.88.4.774

Bibliometric Services | NIH Library. (n.d.). https://www.nihlibrary.nih.gov/services/bibliometrics.

Borghi, J., Abrams, S., Lowenberg, D., Simms, S., & Chodacki, J. (2018). Support Your Data: A Research Data Management Guide for Researchers. *Research Ideas and Outcomes*, *4*, e26439. DOI:10.3897/rio.4.e26439

Cronin, B., & Atkins, H. B. (Eds.). (2000). *The web of knowledge: A Festschrift in honor of Eugene Garfield*. Medford, NJ: Information Today.

Data Citation Synthesis Group. (2013, October 30). *Joint Declaration of Data Citation Principles – FINAL*. Retrieved from FORCE11 https://www.force11.org/datacitationprinciples. Accessed on February 5, 2019.

Fenner, M., Lowenberg, D., Jones, M., Needham, P., Vieglais, D., Abrams, S., ... Chodacki, J. (n.d.). Code of practice for research data usage metrics release 1. DOI:10.7287/peerj.preprints.26505v1

Gutzman, K. E., Bales, M. E., Belter, C. W., Chambers, T., Chan, L., Holmes, K. L., ... Wheeler, T. R. (2018). Research evaluation support services in biomedical libraries. *Journal of the Medical Library Association: JMLA*, *106*(1), 1–14. DOI:10.5195/jmla.2018.205

Hargens, L. L. (2000). Using the Literature: Reference Networks, Reference Contexts, and the Social Structure of Scholarship. *American Sociological Review*, *65*(6), 846–865. DOI:10.2307/2657516

Hicks, D., Wouters, P., Waltman, L., de Rijcke, S., & Rafols, I. (2015). Bibliometrics: The Leiden Manifesto for research metrics, *Nature 520*, 429–43. doi:10.1038/520429a

Hirsch, J. E. (2005). An index to quantify an individual's scientific research output. *Proceedings of the National Academy of Sciences of the United States of America*, *102*(46), 16569–16572. DOI:10.1073/pnas.0507655102

Jaffe, A. B., & de Rassenfosse, G. (2017). Patent citation data in social science research: Overview and best practices. *Journal of the Association for Information Science and Technology*, *68*(6), 1360–1374. DOI:10.1002/asi.23731

Konkiel, S. (2013). Tracking citations and altmetrics for research data: Challenges and opportunities. *Bulletin of the American Society for Information Science and Technology*, *39*(6), 27–32. DOI:10.1002/bult.2013.1720390610

Makar, S., & Trost, A. (2018, October). Operationalizing bibliometrics as a service in a resarch library. *Information Outlook*, *22*(5), 21–32. Retrieved from http://content.sla.org/InformationOutlookContent/1/1/1/1/1/35/Information_Outlook-September-October_2018.pdf

Muller, J. Z. (2018). *The tyranny of metrics*. Princeton: Princeton University Press.

National Information Standards Organization. (2016). *Outputs of the NISO alternative assessment metrics project* (Recommended Practice No. NISO RP-25-2016). Baltimore, MD: National Information Standards Organization (NISO).

Nicastro, H. L., Belter, C. W., Lauer, M. S., Coady, S. A., Fine, L. J., & Loria, C. M. (2016). The Productivity of NHLBI-Funded Obesity Research, 1983–2013. *Obesity*, *24*(6), 1356–1365. DOI:10.1002/oby.21478

Robinson-García, N., Jiménez-Contreras, E., & Torres-Salinas, D. (2016). Analyzing data citation practices using the data citation index. *Journal of the Association for Information Science and Technology, 67*(12), 2964–2975. DOI:10.1002/asi.23529

San Francisco Declaration on Research Assessment (DORA). (2019). https://sfdora.org/

Shumaker, D., & Talley, M. (2009). Models of embedded librarianship: Final report. *Special Libraries Association, 9*.

Sorensen, J. A. T., & Chambers, D. A. (2008). Evaluating Academic Technology Transfer Performance by How Well Access to Knowledge Is Facilitated--Defining an Access Metric. *Journal of Technology Transfer, 33*(5), 534–547. Retrieved from https://libproxy.albany.edu/login?url=http://search.ebscohost.com/login.aspx?direct=true&db=eoh&AN=0993479&site=eds-live&scope=site

Smith, A. M., Katz, D. S., Niemeyer, K. E., & FORCE11 Software Citation Working Group. (2016). Software citation principles. *PeerJ Computer Science, 2*, e86. DOI:10.7717/peerj-cs.86

Tenopir, C., Allard, S., Douglass, K., Aydinoglu, A. U., Wu, L., Read, E., ... Frame, M. (2011). Data Sharing by Scientists: Practices and Perceptions. *PLoS ONE, 6*(6). DOI:10.1371/journal.pone.0021101

Wilsdon, J., Allen, L., Belfiore, E., Campbell, P., Curry, S., Hill, S., ... Johnson, B. (2015). *The metric tide: Report of the independent review of the role of metrics in research assessment and management.* Unpublished. DOI:10.13140/rg.2.1.4929.1363

Index

Academia, 9, 39, 41, 145
Academic
   disciplinary reputation/prestige, 112
   evaluation, 39
   institutions, 127
   journals, 40–41
   libraries, 149
   publications, 48, 52
   research institutions, 128
Academic research impact
   measurement, 39
   ITS, 47–48
   scholarly metrics establishment, 39–44
   tracking and measuring impact for ITS, 48–55
   transportation, 44–46
Accountability, 8, 43–45, 48, 50, 150
Acquisitions unit, 107
Adie, Euan, 7
Administration, 46, 50, 63, 86, 121
Administrators, 9, 11, 46, 55, 116, 121, 124, 140, 145, 148–149
AFI (Altmetric for Institutions), 130–131, 133
Agencies, federal, 59
AIRs, 67–71, 73
Algorithms, 72, 146
Alternative metrics (Altmetrics), 6–7, 16, 41, 63
   application, 30
   articles, 82
   citation and altmetric data, 141
   institution view, 131–136
   JIFs, 128
   NHMLAC, 129
   researcher view, 136–141
   tools, 11, 128–131, 140–141
   value of, 11, 31, 129

Altmerric.org, 7
Altmetric Attention Score, 7, 132, 134, 138
Altmetric badge, 113
Altmetric Explorer, 65, 130
   for Publishers, 113
   tool, 137
Altmetric manifesto, 6
Altmetric.com, 7
Altmetrics (*see* Alternative metrics)
American Chemical Society, 80
American Recovery and Reinvestment Act, 44
Analytics
   Clarivate, 2, 15, 17, 20, 64
   Google, 116–117
   Plum, 7, 63
   web, 1, 112, 147
Anthropology, 127, 139
Application Programing Interface (API), 20, 24–25, 31, 33–35, 67, 70, 72, 144
Applications, 2–3, 6, 10, 20, 73, 114–115
   altmetric, 30, 129
   grant, 39
Approach, ethnographic, 49, 53
Article Impact Reports (AIRs), 67–71, 73, 97–103
Article Influence calculations, 3
Article Influence Score, 3–4
Article level metrics, 3, 130
Artifacts, 127–128
arXiv, 118
Assessment, 43, 52, 60, 146
   multimodal, 45–46
   portfolio, 54
   qualitative, 139
   research, 44, 51, 53, 123

142 Index

Association of University Presses community, 122
Atmospheric modeling, 19
Atmospheric sciences, 19, 21
Author identifiers, 144
Author level metrics, 5, 63
Author profile tool, 5
Authority, 60, 62, 73, 115, 140
Automated filters, 18
Automation, 25
Awards, 73, 107, 112

Becker Model, 8
Benchmarking, 26, 147
Best practices, 120, 143, 148, 150
Bibliographic information, 48, 129
Bibliometricians, 5
Bibliometrics, 1–3, 10, 15–17, 20, 26, 28, 47, 59, 62–68, 71, 114–115, 118, 144, 146
    analysis, 59, 64, 111, 114
    data, 48, 63–64
    at EPA, 62
    evolving needs and assessing resources, 64–65
    indicators, 41, 71, 148, 150
    requests, 62–63
Bibliometrics and REsearch Symposium, 146
BKCI-SSH, 109, 111
Blogs, 6–7, 82, 128, 137
Book Citation Index–Humanities and Social Sciences (BKCI-SSH), 109
Books, 3, 15, 48, 62, 106, 109, 111–113, 129
Bot filters, 9
Bots, 9, 140
Broader impacts, 132
Brownfields program, 60
Buschman, Michael, 7

California Air Resources Board, 47–48
California PATH, 47
California State Legislature, 10, 47

Caltrans, 47–48, 51
Career, scholarly, 6
Cartels, citation, 9
Case studies, 10–11, 18–31
Category, JCR, 71, 80
Challenges, 18, 66–70, 119, 122, 144–145
Chicken littles, 146–147
Citation-based metrics (*see* Bibliometrics)
Citation(s), 4–7, 9, 19–20, 23, 29, 31, 41, 47, 52, 54, 66, 68, 109, 111, 130
    and altmetric data, 141
    analysis, 16, 128
    count, 1, 3–4, 6, 9, 17–18, 20, 23, 29–30, 63, 71, 109–111, 118, 128, 144–145, 150
    data, 2, 4, 40, 52, 63, 65, 72, 111, 147
    databases, 40, 129
    frequency patterns, 4
    indexes, 2, 3, 109, 144–145
    information, 129
    metrics, 9, 18
    networks, 4, 111
    patent, 65–66
    rates, 4, 49
    tracking, 42, 52–54
Cited half-life index, 3
Cited publications, 20, 24, 29, 31
CiteScore, 4, 150
CiteULike, 82
Clarivate Analytics, 2, 15, 20, 27, 64
Clarivate, 3, 34, 40
Clean Air Act (CAA), 60–62
Co-authorships, 66
Collaborations, 15–16, 23, 114, 122–123, 145
Collaborators, 6, 16, 26, 48
Community
    community-owned infrastructure, 122
    community-owned scholarly infrastructure, 105
    software and data products, 28
Community, academic, 7, 44

Compliance, 108, 123
  Deep Blue, 118–119
  journals, 114–115
  monographs, 108–111
Computational Information Systems Laboratory (CISL), 19, 38
Computing, high performance, 18–19, 21
Connected Corridors Program, 47
Connotea, 82
Context-sensitive approach/evaluation, 50, 54
Contextualization, 8, 36, 148
Corporate Average Fuel Economy (CAFE program), 60
CrossRef, 20, 24, 54–55, 82, 123
Curating publication sets, 34
Curriculum vitae, 9
Cuyahoga river fire (1969), 59–60
Cyberinfrastructure, 27, 143

Dashboards, metric, 34, 113
Data
  citation principles, 146
  collection, 22, 25, 30–31, 34–35, 54, 150
  entry, 22, 130, 144
  extraction, 20, 67, 70
  output formats, 143
  projects, 29
  providers, 4, 20, 24, 33
  sources, 7, 17, 33–34, 68, 72, 109, 118, 150
  visualizations, 64, 66, 68
Data Citation Synthesis Group, 146
"Data trust" framework, 123
Databases, 2, 16, 51
  scientific, 72
DataCite, 123
Datasets, 2, 29, 30, 106, 108, 131, 146
De-duplication, 22
Declaration on Research Assessment (DORA), 9, 124, 147

Deep Blue, 105, 107, 117
  compliance, 118–119
  defiance, 119–120
  institutional repository, 105, 108
Deep Blue Repository and Research Data Service, 108
Deep Web, 117
Defiance, 108–109, 123
  Deep Blue, 119–120
  journals, 116–117
  monographs, 111–114
Deployment, 53
Development effort, 119
Digital Science, 109
Dimensions, 7–8, 109–110, 150
DimensionsPlus, 109–111
Disciplines, 143
  academic, 39
Discoverability, 113, 145, 148
Discovery, 16, 64, 118–119, 129, 140, 146
Dissemination, 1, 6, 8, 10, 35, 144
Documentation, 3–4, 50, 54, 66, 69–70, 128
Documents, 22, 52, 62, 62
  technical, 53, 67
DOI (digital object identifier), 19–20, 22–24, 28–29, 51–52, 55, 65, 123, 131, 137, 144, 148
  metadata, 123
Domain
  experts, 16, 24, 26, 33, 149
  specialized, 26
Donations, 131, 143
Donors, 11, 128, 137
Donut, Altmetric, 7

EarthCube, 10, 27
EarthCube community metrics (EC community metrics) (*see also* Site visit team metrics (SVT metrics)), 27
  lessons learning, 30–31
  outcomes, 28–30

EarthCube Science Support Office (ESSO), 27
Ebooks, 112–113
EBSCO Information Services, 7
Economic
  benefit, 8, 42
  impacts, 46
Editors, 107, 114, 116–117, 144, 145
Egghe, Leo, 5–6
Eigenfactor, 3
Eigenfactor Score, 3
Elsevier, 3–4, 7
Elsevier Announces Scopus Book Expansion Program (2013), 109
Emerging research areas, 145
Emerging Sources Citation Index, 114
Employs transparent methods, 114
Encyclopedia of Diderot and D'Alembert Collaborative Translation Project, 108
Energy Star program, 60
English Language Teaching (ELT), 107
Entomology, 139
Environmental Benefits Mapping and Analysis Program (BenMAP), 73
EPA-RTP Library, 59–63
eScholarship, 50–51
eSenate Bill 1 (SB1), 47
Evaluation, 1, 4–6, 52, 72
  academic, 39
  expert, 147
Evaluative process, 9
Excel spreadsheets, 63, 65
Extreme non-normal distributions, 113

Facebook, 82
Faculty, 7, 41, 48, 114, 124
FAST Act, 45, 47, 50
Federal Highways Administration (FHA), 45
Federal RePORTER, 44
FHWA template, 50–51

Field Weighted citation Impact (FWCI), 40
Fields
  emerging, 123, 144
  scientific, 26, 70
Filters
  automated, 18
  bot, 9
Fixing America's Surface Transportation Act (FAST Act), 45, 47
FORCE 11, 146
Formats, 6, 34, 41–42, 52
  new publication, 6
Fostering social cohesion, 42
Fraud, 8–9, 147, 150
Free eBook Supply Chain, 112
Fulcrum, 122
Funded
  agencies, 16, 106, 116, 128, 131, 137, 148
  research, 16, 42, 44
  sources, 66, 131, 143
Funding, 1, 27, 47, 119
  agencies, 121
  grant, 122
  portfolios, 39
  public, 42–43
  scarcity, 42
  sources of parent organization, 143
Future of the History of Chemical Information, The, 3

G-index, 5–6, 65, 71
Gamesmanship, 8–9, 147
Gaming, 43, 140, 147
Garfield, Eugene, 2–3
Goals, 15, 18, 44, 148
  strategic, 17
Google, 49, 117–118
Google analytics, 116–117
Google Books, 109
Google Data Studio (2017), 116–117
Google Documents, 22–23

Google Scholar, 2, 4–5, 9–10, 40–42, 47, 49, 51, 63–64, 65–66, 109, 111, 129, 144, 146
Google Scholar Citations, 5–6, 41, 49, 65
Google Sheets, 25
Government funding, 1
Grants, 27, 44, 47, 60, 107, 109, 131, 143
Gray literature, 41–42

H-index, 1, 5–6, 41, 63, 65, 71, 74, 144, 147, 150
Hathi Trust, 122
Health sciences, 114–115
Higher Education Funding Council, 44
Hirsch's indicator, 5–6
Humanities, 2–3, 10–11, 105, 114, 119, 123
Humanities Open Book Program, 107
Humanities-oriented monograph publishers, 106
HuMetricsHSS, 124

Identifiers, 20, 27, 29, 31, 33, 50, 131, 148
 persistent, 36, 146
 standardized, 144
Immediacy index, 3
Impact, 1, 5, 17, 23
 measuring, 8, 11
 metrics, 1–3, 9–10
 potential, 49, 52
 statements, 143
 Story, 63
InCites, 17, 34, 64–65, 144
Incorporating Google Analytics, 117
Indexes, 2–3, 109, 114–115, 120
 ISI, 2
Indexing, 65, 109, 114–115, 119
 manual, 10
Indicators, 1–3, 6–7, 10, 16, 35
 altmetric, 6, 150
 newer, 150
Influenza Encyclopedia, 108

Infographics, 11
Information, 6, 10–11
 center, 10–11, 143–145, 149
 science, 30, 32, 34, 70, 72, 129, 143
 scientist, 16, 150
Informetrics, 16
Infrastructure, 18–19, 27, 35, 55, 115
INRIX, 48
INSI, 148
Institute for Scientific Information indexes (ISI indexes), 2–3
Institute for Transportation Studies (ITS), 10, 47–48
 considerations and potential steps, 54–55
 documenting PTA/SB1 projects, 50–51
 Google Scholar, 49–50
 Library, 48
 measuring impact for, 48
 tracking PTS/SB1 projects, 51–54
Institutional benchmarks, 143
Institutional repositories, 108, 117
Institutional repository, 105
Institutions, 131–136
 academic, 46, 127–130, 140, 147
Instruction, 62–63, 69–70, 145
Internal staff-intensive process, 129
Internet of Things (), 36
Investment, 42, 44, 114, 121

Joint Declaration of Data Citation Principles, 146
Journal articles, 52, 67, 109, 111, 119, 129
 peer-reviewed, 1, 6–7, 143, 146
Journal Citation Reports (JCR), 63–64
 metrics for top journals, 81
 top journals by JCR category ranking, 80
Journal editors, 114–115, 144–145
Journal Impact Factor (JIF), 1, 39–41, 63, 70–71, 73–74, 114, 147

146 Index

Journal Impact Factors (JIFs), 128
Journal of Criminal Justice (*JCJ*), 9
Journal(s), 106, 114
    compliance, 114–115
    defiance, 116–117
    rankings, 64
    scholarly, 118
    usage metrics, 1
Judgment of experts (*see* Peer review)

Knowledge Unlatched, 107, 121–122

Labor-intensive processes, 144
Laboratories, 15, 21, 30
Law, 46, 50, 149
Leadership, 122–123
    and collaboration, modeling, 105
Leading for change, 120
    community-owned infrastructure, 122
    leadership and collaboration, 122–123
    new business models, 120–122
Level of Service (LOS), 46
Librarians, 11, 62–64, 66–67, 70, 74, 146
Library Information Technology unit, 108
Library/libraries, 10, 16, 35–36, 61
    community, 10, 64, 70
    publishers, 105, 117, 119, 122
    specialized, 10, 61, 149
Limitations, 8, 10, 41, 72, 121, 145, 147–149
Linked data, 7–8, 150
Literature
    scholarly, 68, 111–112
    searching, 62

Management, 17, 21–22, 33, 35, 62–63, 73
Marketing, 74, 136
Marketing & Outreach, 107
Maturity/level of services, 144
Measurements, 8, 50, 85–86, 140, 146, 150

Measures, citation based, 106, 109, 119
Mendeley, 82
Metadata, 7, 18, 24, 28, 33, 35
Methodologies, 48–49, 148, 150
Metric literacy, 145, 147, 149
Metric misuse, 9
Metric Tide, The, 147
Metrics (*see also* Research impact metrics;Scholarly metrics; Site visit team metrics (SVT metrics))
    analysis, 20, 25, 27–28, 30–31, 33, 35
    journal-level, 9, 63–65, 71
    at NCAR library, 17–18
    new, 39–55, 147, 149–151
    tide, 123
    Toolkit, 124
    traditional, 30–31, 74
Michalek, Andrea, 7
Michigan Journal of Medicine, 114
Michigan Publishing, 105, 106, 111
    Deep Blue, 117–120
    future directions, 123–124
    journals, 114–117
    leading for change, 120–123
    monographs, 108–114
    U-M Library, 106–107
Michigan Publishing Services (MPS), 105–108, 116
Michigan Research Experts, 118–119
Mini-AIRs, 69
Mission, 16, 61, 131, 143, 148
Models, computational, 22, 26–27
Money, 46
Monographs, 10, 105–106, 108
    compliance, 108–111
    defiance, 111–114
    publishers, 106, 113
Moving Ahead for Progress in 21st Century Act (MAP-21), 45, 47
Multimodal assessment, 45–46
Museums, 127–128

National Ambient Air Quality
    Standards, 60
National Center for Atmospheric
    Research (NCAR), 10, 15–16
  analysis, 34
  collaborative activities, 23
  fact sheet, 25
  managing, 33–34
  metrics at NCAR library, 17–18
  planning, 33
  reporting, 34–35
  scientists, 16–17
  supercomputer community
    metrics, 18–21
  supercomputer metrics outcomes,
    20–21
National Center for Computational
    Toxicology, 61
National Cooperative Highway
    Research Program
    (NCHRP), 46
National Exposure Research
    Laboratory, 61
National Health and Environmental
    Effects Research
    Laboratory, 61
National Information Standards
    Organization (NISO), 148
National Institute of Standards and
    Technology, 145
National Institutes of Health
    Library (NIH Library),
    44, 145–146
National Risk Management Research
    Laboratory, 61
National Science Foundation (NSF),
    15, 42, 131–132
  site visit team metrics, 21–27
Natural history museum,
    11, 129, 131, 136
Natural History Museum of
    Los Angeles County
    (NHMLAC), 11, 129
Naysayers, 146–147
NCAR Annual Report (NAR), 17

NCAR Library, 15–17
  metrics case studies, 18–31
  scholarly metrics workflow,
    31–35
Network analysis, 4, 72, 145
New business models, 105,
    120–122
"New" metrics, 149–151
News, 82
  media, 130
NIH Library, 145–146
Non-human resources, 18
Normalization techniques, 40

Office of Air and Radiation, 61
Office of Research and Development
    (ORD), 61, 73
Office of Science and Technology
    (), 44
Office of Scientific Research and
    development (), 42
Open access, 8, 10, 114, 120–122
  journals, 105
  monographs, 107
  scholarship, 143
Open Book Publishers (OBP),
    112–113
Open Ebook project, 122
Open peer review, 7–8
Open Syllabus project, 7, 113
OpenSky, 18
ORCID, 54–55, 123, 148
Organization
  benefits for, 149
  peer, 106
  social sector, 50
Original scholarly research, 141
"Out of the box" resources,
    144–145
Outcomes, 15, 18–20, 24, 36, 50
Output, research, 1–2, 8, 11, 15, 41,
    44, 46–47, 54–55, 108, 118,
    120, 131–132, 140–141,
    144, 146, 149–150
Outreach, 127

148 Index

Parent organization, 10, 143, 148–149
Partisan Gerrymandering and Construction of American Democracy (Engstrom), 111
Peer organizations, 106
Peer review, 8, 40, 107, 147
   blind, 8
   journals, 127
   open, 8
   print and online journal, 128–129
   publications, 128
Peer Reviewed Journals, 127
Peer-reviewed journal articles (PRJAs), 1, 6–7, 143, 146
Performance goals, 45
Performance measurement, 45
Performance outcomes, 21
Philosophers' Imprint, 107–108
Planning, strategic, 35, 128
PLoS Medicine, 40
Plum Analytics, 7, 63
"PlumPrint", 7, 72
PlumX, 7, 68
Policies, public, 7, 42
Policy documents, 7, 65, 72, 82, 106, 109, 113, 130, 132
Policy makers, 137
Presentations, 21, 33, 73, 109, 129–130, 136, 141, 146
Preservation, 118, 127
Primary scholarly publishing unit, 105
Pritchard, Alan, 3
PRJAs (peer-reviewed journal articles), 1, 6–7, 143, 146
Process improvement, 26
Process refinement, 26
Product development, 65
   AIR, 68–69
   next cycle of ideation, 67–68
   RIR, 65–67
Productivity, researcher, 6, 48
Programs, educational, 129
Project management, 27, 51
Project-specific publication metrics, 31
Projects, 11, 27, 29–30

Proposal & Award Policies & Procedures Guide (2018), 131–132
PTA (Public Transportation Account), 47–48
PTA/SB1 project, documenting, 50–51
PTS/SB1 projects, tracking, 51–54
Public engagement, 55, 132, 136
Public Transportation Account (PTA), 47
Publication metrics, 22–23, 27–28, 31, 34
Publications sets, 22, 32, 34
Publications-per-dollar, 28, 30
Publications-per-dollar metric, 28
Publishers, 15, 117, 121–122
   scholarly, 111
Publishing, 18, 30, 105, 122
   electronic, 1, 6, 108
   scientific, 40
Publishing peer-reviewed scholarly monographs, 105
Publons, 8
PubMed, 114
Pure science, 1

Qualitative measures, 2
Quantitative measures, 2

Rankings, percentile, 4
Rankings, weighted, 4
ReadCube, 109
REF 2014, 44
References, 52, 65, 66
   cited, 3, 6
Requestors of impact metrics, 145
Research
   activities, 15–18, 43, 48, 50, 127–128, 130, 133, 137
   agenda, 2, 41
   areas, 22, 43, 66, 68, 145
   articles, 67, 108, 119, 129–130, 136, 138–139, 141
   assessment, 13, 44, 51, 53, 123
   centers, 47–48, 51, 55

cycle, 2, 7, 150
data services, 108
dissemination, 8
evaluation, 4, 146, 150–151
findings, 51
funding, 39, 44
groups, 21, 39–40
institutions, 128, 140
library, 34–35
metrics in evaluation, 148
organizations, 11, 15, 30, 33, 35, 39, 61
outputs, 1–2, 8, 11, 15, 41, 44, 46–47, 54–55, 108, 118, 120, 131–132, 140–141, 144, 146, 149–150
portfolio, 53, 55
productivity, 48
programs, 19, 39, 43–47, 49, 51
projects, 7, 9, 39, 43, 47, 49, 53, 106, 129
Symposium, 146
Research Excellence Framework (REF), 43–44, 106
Research impact, 1–2, 39–44, 62–63, 73
services, 11, 59, 62–63, 67, 72–74, 145–146
Research impact metrics (*see also* Scholarly metrics), 1, 71, 106, 108, 114, 120, 124
benefits for greater organization, 149
benefits for information center, 149
best practices, 148
challenges, 144–145
divergence, 143–144
efforts at regulation, 147–148
influencers and sources, 2–3
"new" metrics, 149–151
spread of scholarly metrics in specialized settings, 9–10
Research Impact Reports (RIRs), 65–70, 73, 76–77
Research information management (RIM), 118–119

Research objects, non-traditional, 119
Resource allocation, 1–2
Resource Conservation and Recovery Act (RCRA), 60
Revenue-generating business, 121
Risk and Technology Reviews (RTRs), 62

Samvera Fedora framework, 108
SB-743, 46
SB1, 47, 48, 52–53
Scholarly achievement, 148
Scholarly activities, 16, 35, 70
Scholarly communication, 16
Scholarly impact, 2, 16, 18, 24, 39, 116, 128
Scholarly metrics, 3, 6, 8, 15–16
establishment, 39–44
lessons learning on future of, 35–36
NCAR Library Metrics Case Studies, 18–31
NCAR library scholarly metrics workflow, 31–35
technological enablers of, 36
Scholarly monographs, 105, 107–108
Scholarly output, 5–8, 10, 19, 105, 118–119, 143–144, 146
Scholarly publications, 15, 17–19, 41, 109, 129–130
Scholarly publishing, 52, 62, 106, 117, 121
sustainable, 105
Scholarly Publishing Office (SPO), 107–108
Scholarly research, 35, 127–128, 130, 141, 150
Scholars, 2, 4, 6, 8, 9, 16, 107, 129, 146
Scholarship, 1–2, 16, 36, 62, 105, 108, 113, 116, 120, 122, 143
peer-reviewed, 17
Sci2, 72

Science and Technology for America's Reinvestment Measuring EffecTs of Research on Innovation, Competitiveness and Science (STAR METRICS®), 44
Scientific knowledge, 42, 44
Scientists, 2, 9–11, 16, 23, 61–62, 149
Scientology, 3
SCImago Journal Rank (SJR), 4, 150
Scopus, 2–6, 15, 41, 49, 109, 111, 114–115, 118
Searching, patent, 67
Self-citations, 4
Self-defeating cycle, 114–115
Shepard's Citations, 3
Site visit team metrics (SVT metrics), 21
　high-level metrics profile, 23
　lessons learning, 26–27
　outcomes, 24–26
Social media, 6–7, 16, 28, 128, 130, 136–137, 140, 150
Social Science Citation Index (Garfield), 2–3
Social sciences, 2–3, 10–11, 105, 109, 119, 124, 145
Social sector organizations, 50
Societal impact of academic research, 42–43
Societal impacts, 42–43
Software, 18–19, 22, 25, 27–29
　citation of, 28, 146
Source Normalized Impact per Paper (SNIP), 4
Special libraries, 10
Specialized research impact services, 145–146
Staff skill sets, 144
Stakeholders, 9–11, 26, 32–35, 41, 46–47, 49–50, 52–53, 55, 74, 106, 114, 117, 122, 144, 148–149

Standardized identifiers, lack of, 144
Standards, disciplinary, 6
STAR metrics, 44
STEM fields, 115, 119, 123–124
Subjects/objects evaluation, 143
Supercomputer, 10, 35
　community metrics, 18–21
Superfund program, 60
Systems, 16, 33, 40–41, 54, 109, 119

Technical resources, 144
Technological enablers of scholarly metrics, 36
Technology, 10, 15, 32, 34, 41, 61, 107, 132, 143, 145
Time, 44–45
Tissue distribution and urinary excretion of inorganic arsenic, 93–94
Tool
　analytic, 128
　bibliometric, 10
　evaluative, 150
Toward an Open Monograph Ecosystem (TOME), 107, 122
Toxic Substance Control Act, 60
Traditional citation-based approaches, 147
Traditional modes of publishing, 117–118
Traditional scholarly metrics, 41
Transportation, 44–46
Transportation research, 46, 49, 51–52, 55, 144
Transportation Research Board (TRB), 46, 51
TRID, 51
Twitter, 82, 130, 139–140
Tyranny of Metrics, The, 8

UC Berkeley, 10, 39
UC Los Angeles (UCLA), 39

United States Environmental
    Protection Agency (EPA),
    11, 45, 59–60, 104
  bibliometrics at EPA, 62–65
  Library Network, 61
University Corporation for
    Atmospheric Research
    (UCAR), 16, 18–19, 27
University of California Institute of
    Transportation Studies
    (UC-ITS), 39, 47, 50–55
University of Michigan (U-M), 105
  Library, 106–107, 120
  Press, 106–107
  Transportation Research
    Institute, 108
University of Michigan Press (UMP),
    10, 106–107, 112–113
US Environmental Protection
    Agency's Library at
    Research Triangle Park
    Library (EPA-RTP
    Library), 59
  agency of evolving priorities, 60–61
  article distribution by research
    category, 79
  biases/limitations, 70–72
  bibliometrics at EPA, 62–65
  challenges, 69–70
  citations each year in web of
    science, 78
  future outlook, 72–74
  highest scoring Altmetric
    articles, 82
  JCR metrics for top journals, 81
  product development, 65–69
  RIR, 76–77
  in support of research, 61–62
  top highly cited articles in web of
    science, 83–96
  top journals by JCR category
    ranking, 80
Usage data, 112–113, 117, 122–123
Usage statistics, 106
USDOT, 47, 51, 54–55
User education, 145

Value, 3, 6, 31, 35, 48, 52–53, 117,
    120–121, 131, 136, 140, 149
Variations, h-index, 5–6
Visualization, data, 64, 66, 68

Web analytics, 1, 112, 147
Web of Science (WoS), 3–4, 18, 24,
    40–41, 49, 63–65, 72, 78, 114
  API, 67
  highly cited articles in, 83–96
Webometrics, 6
Wikipedia, 7, 82, 130, 140
Word cloud, 21
Workflow process, 21, 31–32
Workforce development, 42, 55

www.ingramcontent.com/pod-product-compliance
Lightning Source LLC
Chambersburg PA
CBHW071822230426
43670CB00013B/2531